TENNIS, ANYONE?

TENNIS, ANYONE?

FOURTH EDITION

Dick Gould
Tennis Coach, Stanford University

MAYFIELD PUBLISHING COMPANY

Mountain View, California

Library of Congress Catalog Card Number: 84-061923
International Standard Book Number: 0-87484-720-6
Manufactured in the United States of America

10 9 8 7 6 5 4

Mayfield Publishing Company
1240 Villa Street
Mountain View, California 94041

Sponsoring editor: James Bull
Manuscript editor: Elliott Simon
Managing editor: Pat Herbst
Art director: Nancy Sears
Designer: Gary Head
Photographer: Tim Davis
Illustrator: Kelly Solís-Navarro
Production manager: Cathy Willkie
Compositor: Allservice Phototypesetting
Printer and binder: Malloy Lithographing, Inc.

Contents

Preface

It has been over 20 years since the first edition of *Tennis, Anyone?* appeared in 1964. Its popularity over the years can be largely attributed to its simplicity and its no-nonsense learning progressions. It remains the best-selling "how-to-do-it" tennis book on the market today.

Tennis, Anyone? really works! I have found it exceptionally helpful in my own physical education classes for beginners through advanced players. I use it extensively in my methods course and in my teacher-training programs. Many outstanding teaching professionals have begun their careers with *Tennis, Anyone?* as their bible. The teaching techniques presented are easily applied to group situations and have been the basis for many community and camp programs. The drills and training programs are the same as I use with my championship teams at Stanford University.

But how tennis has changed over the last two decades! Dramatic improvements in equipment, a much more scientific approach to conditioning and training methods, the actual tournament structure of tennis itself, evolution of rules and scoring, and even the theories of how to hit the ball have certainly illustrated that tennis is not a static game. The numerous changes have necessitated this new and updated edition.

All new photographs and diagrams are used in this completely rewritten book. The format is made simpler and more attractive than ever. In summary, I truly believe that whether you are a beginning tennis player, a good competitive player, or a teacher of tennis at any level, you will be able to benefit greatly from this new edition. I hope it helps you enjoy tennis even more, whether you are a student or a teacher.

Good luck and have fun!

Dick Gould

The Background of Tennis

HISTORY

Tennis has a rich and intriguing background. Its history has been marred by misfortune, but even kings could not prevent its rise in popularity. The evolution of modern tennis equipment, facilities, and methods has made tennis one of the world's most interesting sports.

Tennis is actually derived from a game similar to handball that was played in ancient Greece, Italy, Egypt, Persia, and Arabia. A wandering minstrel is thought to have introduced the game to Europe by way of the ladies and noblemen of the French court. Indoors the game was played with a rope stretched across the room serving as a net; outdoors it was played across a mound of dirt. At first, the open hand was used to bat back and forth a cloth bag stuffed with hair. Later, an all-wood paddle was used.

In the tenth century, although Louis IV had banned tennis as undignified, the game continued to grow in popularity. In the 1300s, it was again outlawed, this time because Louis X believed that "tennis should be thought of as a Sport for Kings only." In thirteenth- and fourteenth-century France, tennis was known as *jeu de paume* or "sport of the hands." Its current name is probably derived from the French word *tenez*, meaning "take it" or "play."

In the fourteenth century the game moved to England, but there too it had a dubious beginning—outlawed because the king felt his soldiers were wasting time playing tennis that they could be spending practicing archery.

For the next 200 years tennis was played very little. Interest slowly revived in France, England, and other European countries in the sixteenth century. A net replaced the rope cord, and a racket shaped like a snowshoe with strings was developed. Tennis became a more competitive game, and it was common to wager on the outcome of matches.

Edicts banning tennis were published, this time because of the wagering, and the sport again declined in popularity. By the nineteenth century, only the wealthy were playing the game.

The modern history of tennis began in 1873, when Major Walter Wingfield introduced lawn tennis in England. His was a 15-point game in which only the server could score. Called *spharistike* after the Greek root for "ball," it was played on an hourglass-shaped court divided by a net 7 feet high.

Mary Outerbridge introduced tennis to the United States in 1874. A Bermuda vacation gave her the opportunity to see British soldiers playing spharistike, and, in spite of initial difficulty with United States customs officials, she succeeded in bringing rackets, a ball, and a net into this country. She was largely responsible for establishing the first court in the United States—on the lawn of the Staten

Island Cricket and Baseball Club. The sport caught on quickly and developed into a vigorous, fast-moving game of skill.

No one seems to know how the current scoring system evolved, although it is thought that the term "love" probably comes from the French word *l'oeuf*, meaning "the egg" or "zero." There is one theory, however: Early in France, the most common silver piece was worth 60 sous, and each of its four parts was worth 15 sous. Tennis was played for stakes, so points were worth 15, 30, or 45 sous. Eventually, after the coin denominations were no longer significant, 45 was shortened to 40 because it was easier to say.

In 1881, the United States Lawn Tennis Association was founded to standardize rules pertaining to scoring, equipment, and court dimensions. This organization is now called the United States Tennis Association. Today, individual players, schools, recreation departments, cities, and clubs belong to the U.S.T.A., and the popularity of tennis continues to grow.

EQUIPMENT

Rackets

Seldom has the basic equipment in any sport undergone such rapid and dramatic changes as has the tennis racket. For several decades the tennis racket had been almost universally made of wood and of approximately the same size. In the 1970s, however, metal rackets began appearing on the market. By the 1980s, composite rackets were the rule rather than the exception.

Wood rackets have been the standard for years, and they still feature laminations or strips of hard wood, such as maple or ash, glued together to produce a strong product. Wood rackets remain among the lowest priced of today's rackets, with top models selling for more than $50.

A variation of the conventional wood racket uses a *composite wood frame*, in which the wood laminations are reinforced with graphite, boron, or fiberglass to afford added strength and performability. The average cost of such rackets is approximately double that of a medium-priced high-quality wood racket.

Metal rackets are usually made of steel, aluminum, or perhaps titanium. Prices range from the same as for a good wood frame to those of a composite wood frame.

Composite rackets are a more recent addition to tennis racket technology. The frames include varying amounts of fiberglass, graphite, boron, or other fibers, and represent a definite step upward in cost, averaging over $150 per racket.

Many composite rackets have a composition of more than 50 percent graphite fiber and are called *graphite rackets*. These fibers are molded together with epoxy resins to form the racket and thus make such rackets very expensive. Prices in excess of $250 are not uncommon.

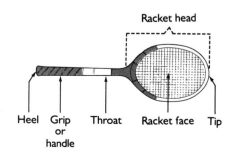

Racket head

Heel   Grip   Throat   Racket face   Tip
        or
        handle

Factors Influencing Which Racket to Buy. Many manufacturers produce several models of each type of racket, and in several price ranges. Certain variables other than price can influence what racket a person buys:

Flexibility: The different models from each manufacturer vary in flexibility, from "rather flexible" to "quite stiff," meaning that some rackets bend at the throat more than others.

Head Size: Rackets may be classified into three head sizes: standard, mid-size, or oversize. The larger the head size, the greater is the hitting area.

Handle Size: Handle grip circumferences vary by one-eighth-inch increments. A small youth may use a $4\frac{1}{4}$-inch or $4\frac{3}{8}$-inch handle. Larger youths or small adults may prefer a $4\frac{3}{8}$-inch or $4\frac{1}{2}$-inch handle. A person with a larger hand might prefer a $4\frac{5}{8}$-inch or even a $4\frac{3}{4}$-inch handle.

Weight: Racket weight can regularly vary from 12 to 14+ ounces. A lightweight racket is 12 to 13 ounces; a medium-weight racket is $13\frac{1}{2}$ to $13\frac{3}{4}$ ounces; a heavy racket weighs 14 ounces or more.

In recent years the trend seems to be toward lighter-weight rackets with smaller handle sizes (both markings—for example, $4\frac{1}{2}$L—are found on the racket), and toward rackets with mid-size or oversize heads. However, personal preference is the most significant factor in choosing the right handle size, racket weight, head size, and even racket composition. Before spending a great deal of money on a racket, be sure to try out several different sizes and kinds. Most large sporting-goods stores and tennis specialty shops have "loaners" for trial use.

Strings

Many "pre-strung" rackets are available at department stores and large sporting-goods dealers, usually employing relatively inexpensive nylon string. Better racket frames are rarely pre-strung; the buyer is able to select both the type and the tension of the strings.

String tension can vary greatly among the different sizes of racket head. Generally, the larger the head, the greater is the string tension. You should ask the store "stringer" for suggestions as to type and tension of strings for a particular racket frame, whether it be to string a new racket, to repair a string, or to completely replace the strings in a used racket. (Strings usually lose some tension after time in the racket.) The *gauge* (thickness) of the string may also be optional to the buyer. Better players seem to prefer a thinner gauge—which provides more "feel"—but a thicker gauge lasts longer.

There are three different types of string—nylon, animal gut, and synthetic gut. Each type has different qualities, and so the types vary in price.

Nylon is the least expensive string, starting around $15, including the cost of installation. It is moisture resistant, but top players don't think it provides the same "feel" of the ball meeting the strings as gut in standard-size or even mid-size rackets.

Natural-fiber *animal gut* is much more expensive than nylon, with prices starting around $30. It consists of around 15 strands of animal intestine fibers twisted together. Oversize racket frames greatly reduce the life of gut strings because with them there tends to be more string movement and thus wear. Also, gut can swell and deteriorate when exposed to moisture. It is, however, the preferred string of top players using standard or mid-size frames.

Manufacturers, spurred on by the need to have a string better suited to oversize racket frames and one that also is much less expensive than gut, have worked hard to develop a superior nylon string. The result is *synthetic gut,* which actually is made not of gut, but of numerous nylon fibers twisted together in a process similar to that used in making natural gut. This refined process and the development of new materials give the nylon string added strength, so it is less subject to breakage or loss of tension in the racket frame. Synthetic gut costs more than monofilament nylon, yet generally much less than animal gut.

Balls

Tennis balls are made of rubber molded into two cups that are cemented together and covered with wool felt. Some balls are covered with extra felt for increased wear and are called *extra-duty balls*. Extra-duty balls are best on courts without too rough a surface (which causes the balls to fluff up) and at higher altitudes. The best balls are inflated with compressed air, which gives them their resiliency. Nowadays, some balls derive at least some of their resiliency from the component rubber. (The extreme example is the "pressureless" ball.) Colored balls, especially yellow ones, are popular for their greater visibility compared to the formerly standard white ball.

Specifications. The official tennis ball, as defined by the International Tennis Federation, is approximately $2\frac{1}{2}$ inches in diameter, weighs 2 ounces, and should bounce approximately 55 inches when dropped from a height of 100 inches.

Care. The container in which tennis balls come packed should not be opened until ready for use, since it is pressure-sealed to help retain pressure inside the ball. Commercial "compressor" cans are available to help pump pressure back into "dead" balls. Since the felt covering of a good ball will wear down, thus making the ball considerably lighter after two or three hard sets, balls are changed every 11 games or so in championship tournaments. For noncompetitive play, however, the life of an otherwise good ball may be temporarily restored by putting the ball through a cycle of a clothes washer and dryer (best done at a commercial "wash center").

Dress

Until recently, the traditional tennis dress was all white, partly because white reflects heat better than other colors. However, tennis fashion is now a thriving business, and colors and coordinated outfits are commonplace. Men wear shorts, shirt (always), socks, tennis shoes (*not* running shoes, which tend to mark the court and often have flared heels that can bring stress to knees and ankles by restricting easy lateral movement), sweater or jacket or warmup suit, and perhaps a cap and wrist band (moisture absorbent, to help keep perspiration from eyes and hands). Women dress the same, except that most women favor either a tennis dress or a skirt and a top.

TENNIS COURTS

Tennis courts come in several types largely determined by the climate and traditions of a particular locale. The court can be indoors or outdoors. Outdoor courts are often surrounded by backdrops of canvas, plastic "saran," a natural hedge, or wooden slats. Such fencing acts to reduce the wind and to increase the visibility of the ball. Indoor courts have made tennis a year-round activity not only in the United States but elsewhere in the world. Rented court time has made indoor centers commercially attractive. Indoor competitive circuits are part of the regular professional circuit. Oftentimes such indoor major events are played in large, general-purpose arenas rather than at tennis centers, and thus "carpeting" is laid down as the playing surface. Whether indoors or outdoors, however, courts may be classified as hard, grass, or soft.

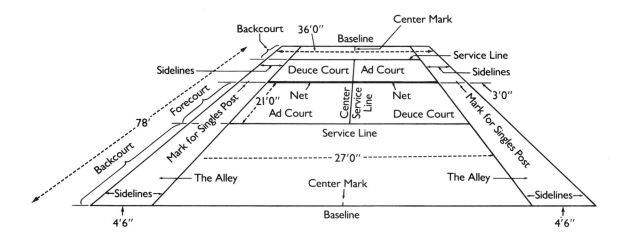

Hard Courts

Courts surfaced with asphalt, cement, wood, or composition materials are classified as *hard courts*. The United States has by far the greatest concentration of hard courts. And the hard court is essentially the only surface found in the western United States.

Advantages. The ball bounces uniformly. A minimum of upkeep is required, although an asphalt court needs to be resurfaced every four or five years. Hard courts are usually colored to facilitate ball visibility, often green with a red border area surrounding the boundary lines.

Disadvantages. The primary disadvantage of the hard court is that it is not standard throughout the world. Some people object to the aggressive style of play that is possible on this "faster" court ("faster" because the ball rebounds rather quickly from the hard playing surface).

Grass Courts

Grass provides a popular and traditional surface, a carryover from the early days when people erected a net and played on the lawns of their estates. In fact, tennis then was called "lawn tennis." Today, grass is the world's least common tennis court surface, though two major international championships—Wimbledon and the Australian—are still played on grass.

Advantages. Most players enjoy tennis on a grass surface. The style of play is more aggressive than on clay, since the ball tends to skid and bounce low. The grass surface encourages net play, partly because of the ever-present possibility of bad bounces.

Disadvantages. Grass courts require constant maintenance. The grass must be clipped smooth and kept watered, and the lines need frequent remarking. When a grass court is damp, the ball becomes heavy and wet, and the court itself is slippery. Where the turf is worn, bounces are irregular and unpredictable. Most touring professionals become impatient with a surface that is so imperfect.

Soft Courts ("Clay")

In areas where grass doesn't grow well, or where composition materials are difficult to secure, dirt or clay is a common court surface. The vast majority of the world's tennis courts are soft courts. The soft court is by far the most common surface in Europe. In the United States, the South, Midwest, and East all have a high proportion of "clay" courts.

Advantages. The soft court is easy on the feet. The style of play is slower, and less emphasis is placed on attack. Since the ball bounces higher and more slowly from the coarse surface, opponents have more time to get to the ball and prepare for the return shot.

Disadvantages. The "clay" court is difficult to keep in top playing condition. It must be watered and pressure-rolled daily, and the playing lines need to be retaped or swept, or rechalked.

Hitting the Ball: The Basic Strokes

In learning to play tennis, several concepts are important.

Relaxation: To help you relax while concentrating on what you are doing, try to slow down all your motions. Thus, when learning to hit a tennis ball, try not to hit hard. Instead, try to feel the ball on the hitting face of the racket. With your wrist firm, try to hold the ball on the racket as long as possible by hitting in "slow motion." Avoid jerkiness and abrupt movements. Develop a hitting *rhythm* by smoothing out the swing as much as possible.

Simplicity: Mechanically, the stroke should be as simple as possible, with no sacrifice of control or power. The more unnecessary movements you make during a stroke, the greater is the possibility that one of them will adversely affect the shot. Most movements in tennis are natural movements—the difficult thing for the learner is to let them be natural.

Repetition: This book constantly emphasizes doing one thing over and over again correctly in order to form a correct habit pattern. First you should know what you did incorrectly, and then—just as important—you should immediately correct your mistake. As far as the basic strokes of tennis are concerned, this makes the finish of each shot extremely important. By *holding your finish* for a second or two, you can observe much of what happened during the hit itself. Then, by *correcting* to the proper finish position, you can mechanically form a habit of repeating the correct swing.

Preparation: The majority of balls are missed because the inexperienced player does not get the racket back soon enough or does not move into position to hit as quickly and efficiently as possible.

Actually, you should be just as concerned with the start of a stroke as with the finish. The stroke will be analyzed here, so you won't have to think about ball contact until you have prepared for the stroke. Then, after ball contact, you should hold your finish so you can analyze and correct your feet, which allows you to have proper balance and in turn permits you to hold the racket in proper position. The premise is: Your chances for hitting the ball well are enhanced if the start and finish are right, since what happens in the middle of the swing will then also be right.

The above-mentioned concepts will now be applied to actually hitting the ball, beginning with the basic forehand and backhand groundstrokes. The presentation is geared to the right-handed player: *Left-handers will have to reverse the terminology.*

THE FOREHAND

First learn the forehand grip on the racket. To get this grip, hold the throat of the racket lightly in your left hand, with the racket face perpendicular to the ground—that is, as if the racket were "standing on edge." The racket is at waist level, pointing to the net. If there were a camera in the heel of the racket, it would take a picture of your belt buckle.

With your right hand, grip the handle in a "shaking hands" position. (The palm of your hand should be almost perpendicular to the ground.) The "V" formed by the juncture of your thumb and index finger is thus squarely on the top side of the racket handle. The thumb is completely around the racket handle, and your fingers are slightly apart.

If you are on a court, face the net and stand a little behind the juncture of the "T" formed by the baseline and the center mark. Place your feet about shoulder width apart, with your weight evenly distributed on the balls of your feet, and with your knees slightly bent.

Move a few inches to the left of the "T," so that you can use the court markings as a reference. From the "set" position, "turn" by stepping with your right foot to the "T," and bring your racket straight back. This puts you in the "ready-to-hit" position.

The racket is still at waist level, with the racket head no higher than your wrist. Pretend you have a camera in the heel of your racket and are going to take a picture of where you want the ball to go.

The Grip

The "Set" Position

The Backswing

Common Faults

- The "V" is positioned too far to either side of the top of the handle.
- The grip is a hammer grip—that is, the fingers are too close together.
- The grip is too limp or too tight.

- The knees are too stiff.
- The body is bent over excessively from the waist.
- The racket head is too high above the wrist.
- The racket points off to the left rather than straight ahead.

- The initial step is back, away from the ball, rather than toward the "T."
- The backswing is started after the body turn, rather than being an integral part of the turn.
- The player fails to turn completely sideways.
- The wrist drags the racket back.
- The elbow gets too far away from the body, preventing the racket from "standing on edge" and leading to excessive wrist movement.
- The backswing is too high, which makes for too much wasted motion.
- The racket head is above the wrist and the wrist is above the waist.
- The arm is too straight and stiff.

Now that you are "ready to hit," transfer your weight into the shot by stepping toward the net with your left foot at about the time the ball bounces. (You will probably have to "adjust" your body position slightly by taking some small, quick steps to enable you to transfer your weight toward the net.) With your wrist firm, contact the ball well in front of your body. Try to "carry" or "hold" the ball on the racket face as long as possible. To help you develop a feel of the ball on the racket, *always hit slowly and softly.*

Always "hold" your finish until you have corrected the following, in order: your feet, your balance, and the racket position.

1. Feet

    a. All your weight is on the front (left) foot, which is flat on the ground and at a 45-degree angle to the net.

    b. The back (right) foot has only the very tip of the toe lightly touching the court, and the back leg has relaxed into a comfortable stance.

    c. An imaginary straight line touching both toes should now extend toward where the ball is to be hit.

2. Balance

    a. The front (left) knee is comfortably bent, but you are standing tall and erect from the waist, with your shoulders level to the court.

    b. The racket swing has pulled your rear hip and shoulder around so that you are now squarely facing the net.

3. Racket position

    a. Your wrist is at eye level and is firm. The racket face is "standing on its edge" so that the imaginary camera in the heel of the racket can take a picture of your left side. The "tip" end of the racket head is pointing toward the top of the fence across the net.

    b. The racket is pointing about 45 degrees beyond where you want the ball to go, which means you will be looking over your elbow after the ball.

The Forward Swing

The Finish

Common Faults

- Lack of "adjusting" footwork has prevented a weight transfer into the direction of the shot.

- The ball is hit too late or the wrist is cocked back, which makes the ball go too far to the right.

- The ball is contacted too close to the body, which tends to make the racket head drop and the swing "scoop" the ball up too high.

- The wrist rolls over, which can make the ball go into the net.

- The wrist slaps at the ball, which brings the tip of the racket head through too soon. This results in too hard a hit or makes the ball go sharply to the left.

- The swing from the ready-to-hit position is down rather than up to the ball.

- The knee is stiff and the body bent over.

- The body opens toward the net too soon.

- Feet

    - The front (left) heel rises off the court or the front foot turns open too much.

    - The weight is transferred sideways— the step is not toward the net.

    - The back (right) foot has not come up to the tip of the toe, so that the sole of the shoe is not facing the rear fence.

- Balance

    - The legs are too stiff, causing the body to bend forward from the waist. (The back leg should be relaxed so that the back foot can slide up some.)

    - The shoulders are not level.

    - The hips are not facing the net.

- Racket position

    - The wrist is not at eye level.

    - The tip end of the racket fails to point into the direction of the hit, and the racket face isn't "on edge."

    - The elbow does not finish in front of the chin.

THE BACKHAND

The backhand stroke is very similar to the forehand in terms of technique and learning progressions. One of the main differences is in how the racket is held. Change to the backhand grip by using your left hand on the throat of the racket to guide it back from the "set" position (so that the camera in the heel of the racket can take a photo of your right hip). Simultaneously, with your right hand make a near quarter turn so the palm of the right hand is essentially on the top of the racket. The inside of the top knuckle of the index finger rests squarely on top of the handle. Your fingers are slightly spread, and the thumb may give added support by being diagonally or at a slight angle down the back of the handle.

If you are on a court, stand a little behind the "T" at the back of the court and face the net. Place your feet about shoulder width apart, with your weight evenly distributed on the balls of your feet, and with the knees slightly bent.

Move a few inches to the right of the "T" from the "set" position. "Turn" by stepping with the left foot toward the "T." Bring your racket back the rest of the way, with your left hand still lightly holding the racket at the throat. Except for the grip, the backhand "ready-to-hit" position is like that of the forehand in that the racket is at waist level, with the racket head no higher than the wrist and the camera in the heel of the racket now taking a picture of where you want the ball to go. However, your hitting arm is comfortably straight and the other hand is still lightly on the racket throat.

The Grip

The "Set" Position

The Backswing

Common Faults

- The top knuckle of the index finger is not positioned on top of the handle.
- The grip is a hammer grip—that is, the fingers are too close together.
- The grip is too limp.
- The grip has not turned enough from the forehand grip.
- The thumb is straight across the back of the handle, instead of at a diagonal.

- The knees are too stiff.
- The body is bent over excessively from the waist.
- The racket head is too high above the wrist.
- The racket points off to the left rather than straight ahead.

- The initial step is back, away from the ball, rather than toward the "T."
- The backswing is started after the body turn, rather than being an integral part of the turn.
- The player fails to turn completely sideways or turns too late.
- The backswing is too high, which wastes too much motion, and the elbow is bent rather than comfortably straight.
- The left hand lets go of the racket too soon.
- The racket head is above the wrist and the wrist is above the waist.

Now that you are "ready to hit," first take some quick adjusting steps; then transfer your weight at about the time the ball bounces by stepping toward the net with your right foot. With your wrist firm, contact the ball well in front of your body. Hit the ball softly by lifting it out toward the net. Slowly let the tip of the racket follow out after the ball.

Always "hold" your finish until you have corrected the following, in order: your feet, your balance, and the racket position.

1. Feet

   a. All your weight is on your front (right) foot, which is flat on the ground and at about a 45-degree angle to the net.

   b. Your back (left) foot has only the very tip of the toe lightly touching the court, and the back leg has relaxed into a comfortable stance.

   c. An imaginary straight line touching both toes should now extend toward where the ball is to be hit.

2. Balance

   a. Your front (right) knee is comfortably bent, but you are standing tall and erect from the waist, with your shoulders level to the court.

   b. The racket swing has pulled your rear hip and shoulder around so that you are now facing at a 45-degree angle to where you want the ball to go (not quite as much of a turn as with the forehand).

3. Racket position

   a. Your wrist is approximately at eye level and is firm. The racket face is in the same plane as your shoulders, and the imaginary camera in the heel of the racket can take a picture of your front (right) foot. In other words, the racket head, due to the nature of the backhand grip, is higher above the wrist than with the forehand.

   b. The racket arm has moved so it is pointed about 45 degrees beyond where you want the ball to go. Your left hand has lightly followed the racket at the start of the swing, so that it now rests just in front of your waist.

The Forward Swing

The Finish

Common Faults

- Lack of "adjusting" footwork has prevented a weight transfer into the direction of the shot.
- The ball is contacted too late, which makes the ball go to the left.
- The tip of the racket comes through too soon, which makes the ball go to the right.
- The ball is contacted too close to the body, which tends to make the elbow bend, the racket head drop, and the swing "scoop" the ball up too high.
- The left arm fails to help initiate the forward swing by not guiding the racket toward the ball.
- The elbow bends (often because the guiding left hand has released the racket too soon), which causes the racket head to rise above the wrist and brings the swing (and ball) down.
- The wrist fails to remain firm, causing the racket head to drop and making the ball go too high.
- The body opens up too much toward the net, often due to late ball contact.
- The ball is hit too hard and abruptly, rather than being smoothly lifted into the direction of the hit.
- Feet
  - The front (right) heel rises off the court or the front foot turns open too much.
  - The weight is transferred sideways. The step is not toward the net.
  - The back (left) foot has not come up to the very tip of the toe.
- Balance
  - The legs are too stiff, which causes the body to bend forward from the waist.
  - The shoulders are not level.
  - The body is facing toward the net too much.
- Racket position
  - The wrist is not approximately at eye level.
  - The racket tip fails to point into the direction of the shot and fails to finish above the wrist.
  - The finish is not far enough around the ball to the right of the body.

THE TWO-HANDED BACKHAND

The Grip

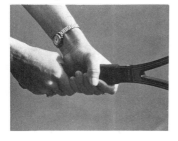

The "Set" Position

The Backswing

If you are relatively small and lack strength in your wrists, or if you have a sore elbow, you may have found that there is less strain on your arm if you hit the backhand with *two* hands holding onto the racket. (Many of the growing number of top players who use two-handed shots today began at an early age and needed the extra hand to give added support to the racket.) In addition to added strength, there are other advantages of the two-handed backhand: a very precise stroke, heavy ball pace and penetration, and a tremendous amount of disguise to the direction of the shot.

However, there are some disadvantages to using two hands. These include:

1. A premium on precise footwork.
2. Possible confusion when learning to volley.
3. Reduced flexibility for spinning the ball, especially for obtaining underspin on approach shots and on serve returns.

In summary, the two-handed backhand may be just right for you. Try both the one-handed backhand and the two-handed backhand to see which feels best. Here are the techniques for hitting the two-handed backhand.

The Mechanics

Most two-handed backhand players hold the racket using their regular forehand grip in each hand, with the right hand at the base of the handle and the left hand higher up on the handle. Two-handed players usually use a fairly straight backswing and always make a complete pivot, since having both hands on the racket pulls the front shoulder well around toward the net.

Footwork is even more critical in two-handed shots than in one-handed shots. If you are late getting to the ball and have to step to the side (parallel to the baseline) to reach it, your back side (left side of the backhand) is prevented from turning into the shot; thus you are forced to rely too much on your wrists to get the racket head through the flight of the ball. Try to position yourself, therefore, to step straight into the line of the shot so that your left hand can help pull your left hip through on the finish.

On contact, try to keep the racket face on the ball for as long as possible by letting the racket tip come around the outside of the ball. To do this, keep the wrists firm, and be certain on the finish that the racket head is not turned over and that the racket and your arms are pointing in the direction of the shot. You can think of the two-handed backhand as a left-handed forehand.

The Backswing

The Forward Swing

The Finish

PRACTICING THE FOREHAND AND BACKHAND

Practice with a Partner

As a beginner, the best way to practice is with a partner who tosses the ball to you as the hitter. The hitter may start at the baseline, with the tosser on the same side of the net. The tosser should toss the ball softly underhand to a spot about 10 feet in front of the hitter. The tosser should only toss when the hitter has completed the backswing and is in the "ready-to-hit" position. The ball should be returned softly so that the tossing partner can catch it at head level (the ball would clear the net by 3 or 4 feet if the partner did not catch it).

Use Adjusting Steps

You will find that even if the tosser has a target at which to toss, the ball is not always where you want it, which makes transferring your weight directly into the shot difficult. Try taking some little "adjusting" steps as the ball leaves the tosser's hand before committing yourself to your final step into the shot. Thus, if the ball is too close, you can quickly adjust back; if it is too far away, you can quickly adjust forward and still step into the hit.

Use "Picture Words"

To help you learn (or if someone else is helping you), "think"—or say aloud—the following words as you stroke:

Turn, meaning pivot and take the racket back to the "ready-to-hit" position

Toss, signaling the moment for your partner to throw the ball

Adjust, meaning take a couple of quick steps to position your feet so you will be able to transfer your weight into the shot

Step and hit, meaning step onto your front foot and then hit the ball

Hold, meaning freeze at the end of the shot in order to see what you did

Correct, meaning correct your feet, balance, and racket position while holding in order to make the correct swing a habit

The Importance of "Holding" and "Correcting"

"Holding" in tennis is important, for it allows you to see what you have done during a swing. By "correcting" what was wrong, a habit for doing the right thing can be formed. Ask your partner to help you with your corrections. *Never* hit the next shot until you have corrected the first.

Since it is difficult to hold the racket in the correct position without being balanced, and since it is almost impossible to have good balance without good footwork, *always* check and correct first your feet, then your balance, then your racket position. In essence, try to become your own teacher.

General Hints

Although you will probably feel restricted and stiff at first, try to develop a soft, slow, fluid hitting motion. Think of a gradual "slow motion" swing—"catching" the ball and "holding" it on the racket, rather than "hitting at" the ball.

As you get a feel for what you are doing and start to develop the rhythm of the swing, have your partner toss a little earlier, that is, as you start to take your racket back, rather than waiting until it is all the way back in the "ready-to-hit" position.

To help develop accuracy and control, try a series of 10 forehand shots and see how many of them you can hit in such a way that you correct your finish and your partner catches the ball. (Your partner should need only one ball if you can consistently hit so it can be caught.) Repeat this test for the backhand as well.

Partner Positions

"Turn": "Toss and Adjust"

"Step and Hit"

"Hold and Correct"

RETURNING WIDE BALLS

The Wide Forehand

You are beginning to feel comfortable returning balls that come close enough so you don't have to run a great distance for them. (We call such returns "adjusting forehands and backhands.") You are gaining more control of the ball and you have little need to correct your finish, since the basic swing has become a habit. Now you are ready to begin hitting forehands and backhands for which you must run a greater distance. Begin by taking a couple of recovery side-skips away from the "T" (to the left for a forehand, to the right for a backhand). Now "turn," by stepping with the foot nearer the direction you wish to go. (The first step is with the right foot for a forehand, the left foot for a backhand.) Simultaneously take the racket back to the "ready-to-hit" position. Run smoothly to the "T." Your partner will toss after you reach the "T," provided you have your weight on the correct foot (the right for a forehand and the left for a backhand) and provided your racket is in proper "ready-to-hit" position. As the ball leaves your partner's hand, "adjust" your feet to the toss before stepping into the shot. Hit and "hold" your finish to *check* and *correct* your feet, your balance, and the racket position. "Recover" by side-skipping back to your original starting point. Remember, however, to always run to the ball with your racket held in back in the ready-to-hit position.

Develop a Practice Rhythm

When you feel comfortable with returning wide balls, and when you are "holding" and correcting well, ask your partner to toss the ball as you near the "T" so that you never have to come to a complete stop before stepping into the hit. (It is important, however, to realize that you, the hitter, must *always* initiate the action. If the tosser tosses before you have turned and started to run, you will have to play "catch-up" with the ball, and you will probably not be able to transfer your weight correctly into the line of the shot.)

You will soon get the feeling of constantly moving. In other words, as soon as you have recovered, push off, turn, and go directly into your next hit. *Always* pause at the finish, however, to make any necessary corrections. In this manner, many balls can be hit in succession in a short time.

Using a Ball Machine

If you use a ball machine, turn, take the racket back, and begin running to the spot the ball will most likely be—all *before* the ball is released. (This gives you, the inexperienced player, time to reach the ball without being hurried.) "Adjust" your feet while the ball is in the air, and "hold" and "correct" the finish before recovering back to the starting point. When you first start out, set the machine for a fairly slow ball and long time interval between shots. Try to develop a rhythm on shots, and make all of them smooth.

The Wide Backhand

RETURNING DEEP BALLS AND SHORT BALLS

The Deep Forehand

To return a high, deep ball, you must move back. To return a short, low ball, you must run in. To practice moving back and in, use the "T" as your home base. Your partner may now alternately toss a high, deep ball that lands just inside the baseline, and a soft, short ball that lands just beyond the service line.

The Short Backhand

The Deep Ball

For the *deep ball,* step back as you turn (onto the right foot for the forehand, onto the left foot for the backhand). The object is to run far enough back to allow the ball time to descend to waist level from the peak of its bounce before you hit it. Since you are now further back in the playing court, you must return the ball higher so it will float deep. That is, you will be hitting a ball that approximates a lob, a ball that arcs quite high above the net.

Take your racket back to a "ready-to-hit" position lower than normal. Do this by leaning slightly backward, thereby lowering your rear shoulder (right shoulder for the forehand, left for the backhand). Point the heel of the racket up toward where you want the ball to go. This should put the racket head slightly below your wrist and permit you to hit up to the ball.

Have your partner toss high as you start back, to give yourself time to adjust your feet and still be able to step into the line of the shot. Lift the ball up so it arcs across the net and "falls down" to your partner. "Hold" your finish and "correct" any faults.

The Short Ball

Now start moving forward for a *short ball*—the next in the sequence—by taking the racket halfway back to the "ready-to-hit" position and stepping forward (with the right foot for a forehand and the left foot for a backhand). Your partner tosses short and you turn the rest of the way. Adjust your feet and step into the shot. (Since the short ball is usually also a low ball, lower the racket head in the "ready-to-hit" position to slightly below the wrist, as you do on a deep ball.) Hit by lifting the ball up to your partner, and "hold" and "correct" the finish.

Use a Steeper Ball Trajectory

Both the deep ball and the short ball must be returned at a higher trajectory than normal—the deep ball in order to carry it deep, the short ball in order to clear the net. Aim to contact the bottom of the ball by starting the swing not only with the racket head lower than usual and below the wrist (and, in turn, below the ball), but also by beveling the racket face slightly open (perpendicular to the anticipated flight of the hit ball). (Remember that the heel of the racket at the completion of the backswing points up into the trajectory you want the ball to take.)

THE PRACTICE RALLY

By returning only one ball at a time, you have as long as you need to correct each shot. However, as you form habit patterns and gain confidence in your ability to correctly hit and control tossed balls, you are ready to move into the more realistic situation in which you return balls that are *hit* to you. This is a most important stage of your stroke development, for if you are careless or are over-anxious to return the ball, you will forget all that you have practiced with tossed balls.

The practice rally is presented in three learning progressions—starting the rally (one-hit rally), returning the ball (two-hit rally), and keeping the ball in play (forever rally).

The Practice-Rally Position

The Practice-Rally Position

Start up close—about 50 feet from your partner. (If you are on a tennis court, stand on the opposite side of the net from your partner and just beyond the service line.) Standing up close rather than "full court" helps you remember to hit softly and gives you time to "correct" your finish before the ball can be returned.

Since most balls hit by beginners are forehands, the forehand rally is emphasized here. If you are on a tennis court, use the alley as your target, and stand outside the alley so that if the ball lands in the alley it will be to your forehand. Or, use the service court, but stand off center so that most balls landing in the service square will be to your forehand. This allows you to prepare early and without hurry, and means you are able to take the racket back to the ready-to-hit position before your partner hits the first ball. As a hitter, your objective is to hit the ball so it approximates a tossed ball moving in a soft arc (rather than a beeline) and so it goes up and then "falls down" into the alley, well short of an imaginary extension of the service line.

Starting the Rally (One-Hit Rally)

Starting the Rally

Turn and take your racket back to the ready-to-hit position. When the racket is completely back, toss the ball up so it bounces in front of you toward the net. When the ball leaves your hand, quickly take a couple of "adjust" steps to ensure that you can transfer your weight into the line of the shot. Softly hit the ball up into your partner's target area and "hold" and "correct" your feet, balance, and racket position. Your partner can gain valuable practice in judging the ball by taking the racket back when you do, adjusting the feet quickly to your hit, and then getting into position to step into the hit ball and catch it with the free (left) hand. If the ball comes high, the hitter learns to adjust back and let the ball drop down. If the ball comes low, the hitter learns to bend the knees in order to catch it at waist level. If the ball is to either side, the hitter gets practice by adjusting either away from or toward the ball. "Play catch" with your partner in this manner until you can control the speed and trajectory of the ball and yet always "hold" and "correct" the finish.

Hints for Controlling the Ball

To help yourself hit softly in an arc: In the ready-to-hit position lower the racket head slightly below your wrist by lowering your back (right) shoulder. Start with your hitting arm slightly bent at the elbow and held so the imaginary camera in the heel of the racket takes a picture of where you want the ball to clear the net. Toss the ball up so it bounces high and allows you to hit it from underneath. Step forward and let your front (left) knee bend while standing straight from the waist up. Follow through completely but slowly.

To help yourself control the direction of the hit, with a firm wrist try to feel the ball on the racket face as long as possible—"push" the ball into the direction of the hit and don't be in a hurry to follow through. Set a goal: See how many of 10 balls you can softly hit within the target area and with a good finish.

Returning the Ball (Two-Hit Rally)

Once you and your partner can control the speed and direction of the one-hit rally (for example, regularly hitting most of the 10 shots into the target area), you are ready to progress to the two-hit rally. Both you and your partner "turn" and take your rackets back to the ready-to-hit position at the same time, as in the one-hit rally. Hit the ball softly to your partner, who returns it if it lands in the target area. "Hold" your finishes and "correct," especially to see if you have "adjusted" your feet to allow yourself to step into the flight of the ball. (Let the ball go by if it comes back to you.) Practice until you and your partner can complete at least 10 successful two-hit rallies.

If you wish to try some backhand returns, adjust your ready-to-hit position so the ball will most likely go to your backhand. If your partner is starting the rally by hitting into the alley, you should move to the other side of the alley so the ball will be to your backhand.

The Cross-Court, Two-Hit Rally

Try a cross-court, two-hit rally. Instead of using the alley and hitting straight ahead, use the diagonally opposite service square as your "target" area and hit across the court. To prepare, emphasize turning to the ready-to-hit position so your side and shoulders are diagonal to the cross-court service square. Toss the ball so you can adjust your feet to step diagonally toward the cross-court target area rather than straight ahead toward the net.

Keeping the Ball in Play (The "Forever" Rally)

It should be an almost natural progression from the two-hit rally to "keeping the rally going." As long as you are not hurried, and as long as the ball lands in the target area (either the alley or the service square), return the ball to your partner. Try for a three-hit rally, and if you achieve it, return the ball for a fourth time, and so on. Emphasize having your racket back *before* the ball lands on your side of the net, but "hold" your finish (and "correct" if necessary) until your shot lands on the other side. (Since you are hitting almost all forehands, there is no need to come back to the "set" position after each shot. If, however, the ball should go to your backhand, and you have the time, return it with a backhand shot.) See how many times you can hit in succession. Gradually move back to full court, hitting softly and with some arc. At this point, the receiver of the first ball should wait in the set position.

Rallying with the Backboard

After you have had some practice with the "forever" rally, a backboard may be used to advantage. The same principles apply: Don't hit too hard; and first practice only forehands, then only backhands (without returning to the "set" position). Hit to a target, such as a chalk mark on the wall. You may wish to let the ball bounce twice to give you more time to prepare.

Two-Hit-Rally Position

Cross-Court Rally

Full-Court-Forever Rally

Using the Backboard

THE SERVE

Practicing the Serve

You should begin practicing the serve at least by the time you have started the one-hit rally. In many ways the serve is simpler than the forehand or backhand because the ball is not moving fast at you or away from you; instead, it is controlled by you. Practice is also easier, for you can do it alone, without a partner. If you are not near a court, you can draw a circle on a wall about 4 feet from the ground, stand about 40 feet away, and hit to the target.

Most of the people who find the serve difficult to learn are those who fail to think of the serve in progressive steps. For example, it is hard to throw the ball up correctly if you are already worrying about dropping the racket behind your back. It is hard to drop the racket if you are thinking ahead to the contact itself. Thus the serve presentation is divided into two parts—(1) the serve toss and backswing and (2) the forward swing (the hit itself).

Start in the "set" position, with your left side toward the net, your weight on the back (right) foot, a forehand grip on the handle, with your left hand cradling the throat of the racket, the racket pointing to where you want the ball to go.

The "Set" Position

Common Faults

- The grip tends to a "hammer" grip rather than a forehand grip. (Actually, as you improve, you should gradually move the grip to something in between a forehand and backhand.)
- The weight starts on the front foot.
- The ball is held in the palm of the hand, rather than with the thumb and the first two fingers.

Let both arms drop together toward your front (left) leg. Use these "picture words": "Both arms down together." Now concentrate on the toss.

Both Arms Drop

- The left hand has lowered to a position beside the front leg rather than in front of it, thus preventing the arms from rising together.

Transfer your weight onto your left foot as your left arm begins to extend up for the toss and as the racket starts to travel past your toes in a wide arc toward the fence behind you. As your left arm reaches up, release the ball. Toss the ball about 2 feet above your extended left hand and about 6 inches in front of your left toe. Use these "picture words": "Now, weight forward and toss."

To check the accuracy of your toss, let the ball drop back down into your outstretched left hand. Hold this position long enough to be certain that your weight has transferred forward onto the front left foot and that the racket arm is extended back with the palm of the hand facing down. "Correct" into the proper position, if necessary.

Weight Transfer and Ball Toss

- The ball toss is too low, because the left arm does not follow through high enough on the toss.
- The ball toss is too far back, because either the weight didn't transfer forward on the toss, or the left hand flicked the ball instead of "placing" it in the air.
- The arc of the backswing is cramped, because the racket wrist turns over on the backswing, causing the elbow to bend before it reaches shoulder level.
- The backswing is not in the hitting plane. In other words, the tip of the racket head fails to point to the fence behind the hitter.
- The backswing and ball toss are hurried, probably because the server is prematurely concerned with ball contact.
- The hitting elbow is not at shoulder level and the tossing arm is not extended fully up at the conclusion of the backswing.

Now, after catching the toss and checking to be certain the racket arm is in the correct position, continue to take the racket back and up into the "ready-to-hit" position by letting the racket arm bend at the elbow. (Thus the racket arm is bent about 90 degrees at the elbow, which permits the tip end of the racket to be pointing straight up.)

The racket now drops behind your back as the elbow moves forward in a "throwing motion."

"Picture words" for the forward swing describing the racket drop and ball contact are "Drop and hit."

The "throwing motion" continues as the racket arm extends upward to contact the imaginary ball and as the wrist snaps up into the hit.

Continue the follow-through out into the direction of the hit and then down to your left side. Balance by letting the back heel come off the ground and by letting the back leg relax as the back foot turns.

Make this entire throwing motion as smooth as possible. Keep repeating this motion in two parts—(1) the backswing and ball toss and then (2) the forward swing.

Now, instead of catching the ball, continue the swing and softly hit the ball. Remember to hold the finish, and balance.

"Ready to Hit"

The Racket Drop

The Hit

The Finish

Common Faults

- Instead of bending the elbow to get the racket high enough to drop, the wrist turns over, thereby preventing a smooth, full transition from the backswing into the forward swing.

- The racket does not drop far enough behind the back. (Think of having, or try to have, the wrist touch the shoulder before hitting the ball.)
- The right side turns forward too soon. (To help prevent this, let the tossing arm drop across the chest.)

- The throwing or hitting motion is cramped. (Be sure to reach up high to hit, and don't let the ball drop too low.)
- The hitting motion is down to the ball rather than up. Not enough wrist action is used.
- The hit is too hard and doesn't have enough arc, which means the body is not relaxed and the swing not loose enough. This causes the body to "muscle" the serve. (Actually try to hit the ball upward.)

- The body falls off balance, probably because the left foot does not stay anchored flat on the ground or because the back leg is stiff and the back foot has not turned. (Keeping the right foot back forces you to hit only good tosses, for the foot cannot step out to reach a bad toss. It also helps give you the proper rhythm of the racket-drop and shoulder-turning action up into the hit.)

NET PLAY

You are now ready to begin net play. For practice you will need a partner but not necessarily a tennis court. First a discussion is presented on forehand and backhand volleys and then on the overhead. For the volleys, you and your partner should stand about 10 feet apart (on opposite sides of the net if you are on a court). Start net play in the "set" position, with the racket head at chest level and your arms slightly forward. The volley is divided into two parts: the preparation and the hit.

The Forehand Volley

To prepare for the forehand volley, step forward with the right foot as you push the palm of your racket hand forward (letting go of the racket with the other hand). Turn your body slightly so you are facing the racket squarely. You should be slightly sideways to the net, with the racket face now approximately parallel to the net and the racket head slightly above your wrist and well in front of your chest. You should be bent slightly forward from the waist. Your hitting elbow is well in front of your body.

When you have prepared by "showing" the hitting face of your racket to your partner, your partner softly tosses underhand to the racket face. For the hit, step toward the ball with your left foot and "block" the ball back toward your partner's head, keeping your wrist firm. Use the step and the elbow action for power.

"Hold" the finish and check to see that your racket face is still almost parallel to the net and the racket head still above your wrist. (The tip end of the racket head should be slightly forward.) Your weight is all on the front foot, with the toe of the back foot lightly touching the ground.

The "Set" Position

The Preparation

The Hit

The Finish

Common Faults

- Elbows are against your side. (The arms should be comfortably forward so that the elbows are in front of the body.)
- The racket head is too low.

- Too much backswing is used, which causes the ball to be contacted late and not in front of the body. (Remember to prepare by keeping your elbow in front of your body.)
- The racket is too high (almost vertical to the ground), which will make low balls go into the net.

- The wrist fails to remain firm on contact, which causes the racket head to drop below the wrist on the finish.
- Don't rush your volley practice. Be certain to do the volley in two parts: the preparation and the hit. Your partner tosses only after the preparation has been completed.
- Don't lunge at your volleys.

- The racket head drops below the wrist after contact.
- The racket face "slaps" at the ball. It fails to remain almost parallel to the net after contact.
- If the ball is low, you bend over too far from the waist and not enough from the knees, causing many balls to go into the net.

The Backhand Volley

Prepare for the backhand volley by pushing your right hand forward as you change grip. (This puts the racket basically parallel to the net, so the racket face is now in position to hit the ball.) At the same time, shift your weight onto your left foot and turn to face the racket squarely. You should bend forward slightly from the waist so your head is close to the racket.

Now your partner tosses to the racket and you step onto your right foot, toward the ball. Keep your left hand still, but with your right arm push the racket forward, holding your wrist firm, to hit (or "block") the ball back toward your partner's head.

"Hold" the finish and check to see that the racket head is still above the wrist. (The tip end of the racket head should be slightly forward.) All your weight is on the front foot, with the toe of the back foot lightly touching the ground.

Some value can be gained by practicing the volley against a wall. Stand 4 or 5 feet from the wall and volley the ball up against the wall. Hit *softly* and hit either forehands or backhands—*not* both. (Don't return to the "set" position.) This is a good way to practice footwork and to set the habit of keeping your hitting elbow and the racket in front of your body.

The Preparation

The Hit

The Finish

Volley Practice

Common Faults

- You forget to change your grip.
- The racket does not stay away from and in front of the body.
- The left hand lets go of the racket too soon.
- The body does not turn enough.

- The ball is contacted late (too close to the body).
- The "swing" is not enough from the shoulder. (The forehand volley relies more on the elbow joint.)

- The racket head drops below the wrist after contact. (The wrist must remain firm.)
- The player bends too far forward from the waist, which tends to make low balls go down into the net.

- The player volleys the ball down rather than slightly up, which makes it impossible for the ball to rebound from the wall back into the hitting position.
- The player swings too much and too hard. (Against a backboard there is only enough time for light hits.)
- The player fails to keep the ball to only the forehand side or only the backhand side. (Again, there is only enough time for one or the other kind of shot, but not enough time to interchange shots.)

The Overhead

For the overhead shot, your tossing partner should be about 10 feet away from you but should stand off to the side so the hit ball does *not* go back to where it was tossed. The ball should be tossed underhand so it goes high and almost straight up, which gives you time to "adjust" your feet to the ball. The overhead is also practiced in two parts—the preparation and the hit.

To prepare, take a step back with your right foot (turning your left side toward the net). Pick your racket straight up from the "set" position to a position similar to the serve ready-to-hit position. (Your hitting elbow should be at shoulder level, and your arm should be bent so the racket is above your head.)

When you are in the ready-to-hit position, the ball is tossed. "Adjust" your feet by sliding forward if the ball is short, or by sliding back if the ball is deep.

For the hit itself, transfer your weight onto the front foot and let the racket drop only a little behind your back (to the shoulder blade) as the hitting shoulder turns forward. Bring your racket forward and up to contact the ball. Use a firm snap of the wrist to hit the ball. Keep the follow-through short, almost as if "tapping" the ball.

"Hold," to see that your weight is balanced on your front foot, the back toe turned, and your wrist "broken," with the racket head tip pointed down in the direction of the hit.

Practice Position

The Preparation

The Hit

The Finish

Common Faults

- The tossing partner does not stand off to the side when tossing.
- The toss is not high enough to give the hitter time to "adjust" the feet to the ball.

- The player forgets to turn sideways.
- The hitting elbow is not up at shoulder level in time.
- The player neglects to adjust the body position to the ball. (Don't get set too soon. Good foot movement is a key to a good overhead. Try catching a few tossed balls while in the ready-to-hit position to check your body position.)

- The player tries to hit the ball too hard and overswings.
- The player neglects to use a good wrist snap.
- The player pulls the head down and thus takes the eyes off the ball, which commonly occurs when the ball gets behind the player or drops too low.

- The player uses too much follow-through and thus neglects the wrist snap.
- The player is off balance and thus brings the back foot around. (The player must learn to hit with the racket head and not with the body.)
- The player dips one of the shoulders instead of keeping them level.

Hitting the Ball: More Advanced Stroke Considerations

There is no magic point in your tennis development at which you should begin learning stroke refinements and additions. The more you practice and the more you play, the quicker you will master the basic forehand and backhand drives, the basic serve, and the basic net shots. You will probably also develop personal style idiosyncrasies, which may differ from the text presentation already given.

Your stroke will develop more rhythm, and you will probably begin using a more fluid ("circular") backswing on your groundstrokes. As you gain confidence, you will begin to hit the ball harder. So that you don't lose control of the harder-hit ball, you will need to give it more spin—more overspin (topspin) and even underspin on the groundstrokes, and sidespin and topspin on the serve. On the forehand, for example, you may find yourself turning your basic forehand grip ("Eastern" grip) a little more to the right on the racket handle ("semi-Western" grip). This makes it a little easier to get additional topspin and will result in a circular backswing, with a slightly closed racket face. To get spin on the serve, you will turn your basic forehand grip a little more toward your left, so it is slightly toward a backhand grip ("Continental" style).

Tactically, you should have to concentrate less on keeping the ball in play, and you should be able to put more emphasis on attacking. Realize that the basic strokes are only a means to an end. Much more important in determining success will be how the strokes you develop are used in a playing situation. However, to prepare for our discussion of singles and doubles tactics (Chapters 5 and 6), let us look at variations of the basic strokes, beginning with backcourt play. A discussion of variations of the basic serve, subtleties of the serve return, and a more detailed description of the mechanics of net play will follow.

BACKCOURT PLAY

The Forehand

The Circular Backswing

In Chapter 2, a straight backswing was presented. It is simple to execute and is certainly adequate for the beginner. As you gain more experience, however, you will become less mechanical in producing your stroke. As you try to use more overspin, realize that the racket cannot simply follow directly into and through the flight of the ball, but must of necessity start a little lower and finish a little higher. A straight backswing can limit this needed flexibility.

It is easy to learn a circular backswing. Begin in the "set" position, with elbows bent so the racket head is at chest level (as for a volley). When you turn, first "think" the tip end of the racket head back (in other words, don't let your wrist drag the racket back). Your arm should be relaxed at the elbow, although the elbow remains comfortably close to the body. Coordinate the backswing with the turn and the pivot so they occur together. Your arm should be relaxed at the elbow so the motion is fluid and circular.

When you have brought the racket all the way back, the racket head should be up near the shoulder, since the arm is not yet straight and you can still run comfortably with the racket in this position.

As you transfer your weight into the hit, your arm straightens a bit, to allow the racket to drop into hitting position below the ball. Dropping the racket head in an uninterrupted motion below the ball may take a little longer, but you will soon sense the basic rhythm and be able to adjust your timing. The racket drop gives the swing an inherent rhythm as well as speed. It also makes it easier to adjust to the lower ball. How far the racket drops depends simply on how low the ball is and how much topspin you wish to put onto the return.

As the swing continues, the racket head comes forward and up to the contact point.

The Backhand

Using Spin on Groundstrokes

In throwing a ball, perhaps you have noticed how much you can make the ball curve by throwing it with spin. In tennis the ball can easily be hit so as to give it spin. In fact, the basic forehand and backhand drives as previously presented will produce a certain amount of overspin (topspin). Such spin can be used to the hitter's advantage to gain more control. This is necessary, for as the ball is hit harder, the force of gravity is less effective in pulling the ball down to the court.

Topspin (or Overspin) Groundstrokes

Topspin can be put on the ball by swinging from low (waist level or below) to high (head level or above). The resultant spin allows the ball to clear the net higher and yet still drop quickly into the playing court.

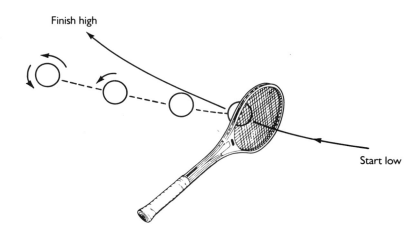

Finish high

Start low

The more topspin you use, the more the ball tends to drop short. Additional topspin may be advisable when playing on a "slow" court, such as clay, where deep shots are not so important (your opponent is less likely to attack the net on a short ball), and where longer backcourt rallies are common. More topspin is needed when you wish the ball to drop or dip quickly, such as when you want to pass the opponent at the net or hit the ball sharply over the net player's head (a "topspin lob").

To gain this additional topspin, start the forward swing even lower. For example, the racket head can begin its forward swing from a position considerably lower than the wrist and with racket face more "closed" or flat. The finish can be higher, meaning a steeper trajectory on the forward swing. In fact, the wrist can even "roll over" the top of the ball on contact (this is common among players who use a semi-Western forehand grip).

The Semi-Western Forehand

Semi-Western Grip

Start Lower

**Finish Higher
(with Wrist Roll)**

The Backhand Slice

Underspin Groundstrokes

The forehand is almost always hit with overspin. But overspin is not the only spin used for groundstrokes. It is just as natural to hit the backhand with backspin, or "underspin." Top players commonly use underspin on backhands when rallying from the backcourt. The underspin shot also affords control. Since the racket head starts to move forward from a position above the ball rather than first having to drop below the ball, the swing is much shorter. A primary advantage of the underspin shot, then, is easier timing, especially when taking the ball on the rise, such as on an approach shot. In addition, the ball does not have to be hit so far in front of the body, an advantage when you are hurried. The underspin ball can be hit with a great deal of pace and penetration, as on a "slice," or it can be hit so softly that it tends to die on the court, as on a "drop shot." The underspin ball does not curve or dip downward as fast as with topspin, so the underspin is not nearly as effective as a passing shot against a net rusher.

How to Slice

For the slice, the racket starts high (at shoulder level), with the racket face beveled "open." The swing is forward and down, out through the flight of the ball. The wrist stays firm and the follow-through is still high, with the wrist at eye level and the racket face still beveled open. It is important to bend your knees so as to bring your body down to the level of the ball. This keeps you from chopping down at the ball.

The Drop Shot

The drop shot is another variation of underspin. This shot softly clears the net and lands short in the court. It is used to pull the opponent to the net or even to produce an outright winner if the opponent is too deep in the court.

For the drop shot, the racket starts well above the wrist and the backswing is very short. The forward hitting motion is down and under the ball. As the racket comes under the ball, open the racket face more, so the ball is given a slight upward and forward lift; yet keep the wrist firm. The racket finishes at eye level, with the face still beveled open.

The trajectory of the swing is much steeper than with the slice, since pace and ball speed are actually negative factors on the drop shot.

The Forehand Drop Shot

THE SERVE

Using Spin on the Serve

As you get more comfortable with the basic serve, you will find yourself gradually hitting harder. If your more powerful serve results in your no longer getting seven out of ten serves consistently in the court, you must learn to put some spin on the ball. All good players spin almost all their serves, because for a small sacrifice in power, they gain considerable consistency. The spin allows the ball to clear the net higher, yet still drop quickly on the other side.

The Spin-Serve Grip

The first thing to do in learning the spin serve is to change the basic forehand grip to one more toward the backhand, sometimes called the "Continental" grip. This grip allows you to brush up along the side of the ball more easily, rather than meeting it "flat on." Your first serves with this grip will probably land short and to the left. Don't get bogged down with swing and hitting details. Simply try to hit up on the ball more, and hit it more to the right. This will give you a wrist hitting action that allows you to "brush" up and across the backside of the ball and results in a spin serve. Initially, you might try serving into a fence or backboard so that you aren't concerned only with results.

The Spin-Serve Ball Toss

The spin serve is divided into two parts: the backswing (including the ball toss and the leg action) and the forward swing. During the ball toss, the body turns sideways more than it does for the basic flat serve. This causes the tossing arm to make a letter "J" motion. The tossing arm will be rising parallel to the base line and pointing less toward the opponent. As you toss the ball, bend both knees forward; this has the effect of causing your heels to rise up from the court. The racket is now up and poised in a "ready-to-hit" position.

Different wrist hitting actions are used for the following three types of spin serves—the topspin serve, the American Twist, and the slice serve. They will be discussed now.

The Ball Toss

The Backswing

The Topspin Serve

The topspin serve is popular because the same basic hitting action is used for both a first serve or a second serve. Generally, a first serve is hit with more pace and less spin, since the server has a second chance to get the ball in the court. A second serve must still be hit with authority but needs more spin to give the ball a better chance of landing in the court. The discussion will begin with the ball toss, which is made to a slightly different spot than in the basic flat serve or even in the other kinds of spin serves.

Toss the ball a few inches in front of the baseline but slightly over your front shoulder (if it were to drop, it would land in front of your heel instead of in front of your toe). Allow the ball to fall a couple of inches from its peak. After the racket has dropped down behind your back, push up with your legs and swing the racket upward to meet the ball. (Think of "brushing" up across the back of the ball with the racket.) As you contact the ball, reverse the wrist so the tip end of the racket goes forward, over the top of the ball. (Concentrating on the racket tip helps to give the ball extra pace.)

You will now be a little off balance, so let the right leg fall across the baseline into the playing court on the finish. This, in turn, will result in the finish being to the body's left. The left arm should be tucked across the body. (The back shoulder comes forward later on the topspin serve than on the flat serve.)

To help learn the proper wrist action, practice the spin serve into the backhand side of the court. Also, don't let your wrist open up so that the palm of the hand faces the sky on the backswing. If this happens and the wrist "breaks" prematurely, you will hit under and around the ball rather than up over the top of it.

The Forward Swing

The American Twist

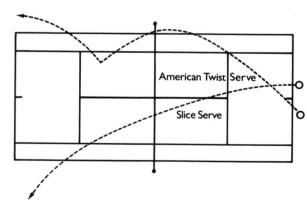

The American Twist Serve

This is an extreme version of the topspin serve. The ball is tossed even farther behind the body, causing the body to bend farther back to reach it and creating an extreme "hitting up and over" reverse wrist action on the ball. This increased hitting up on the ball tends to make it kick up higher after it bounces. Since the ball is tossed farther behind you and therefore hit more on the inside of the ball, the wrist reverse makes it curve into the receiver as it approaches and then kick away in the opposite direction after it bounces. (This serve can create a strain on the back. It is also not used much today, primarily because the excessive topspin tends to make it land short in the receiver's court.)

The Slice Serve

This sidespin serve is quite important, for it allows the right-handed player to serve wide into the receiver's right-hand service square (deuce court), and it allows the left-handed player to serve wide into the receiver's left-hand service square (ad court). It is distinctly different from the topspin serve in that the hit is around the outside of the ball rather than up the inside. Surprise is the key element. Although the easiest way to hit around the outside of the ball is to toss the ball to the right, this also makes it easier for your opponent to "read" what you are planning to do. Thus, try to hit around the outside of the ball by tossing the ball more forward. A common fault is to pull down on this serve. Make sure you keep your head and body up as long as possible during the hit. Also, when practicing the serve, don't be afraid to serve the ball too wide by using extra spin.

The Slice Serve

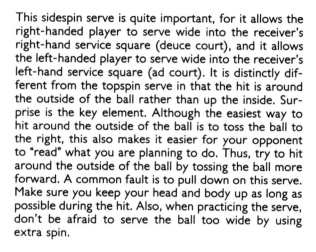

American Twist Serve

Slice Serve

RECEIVING

The Drive Return

The Serve Return

The use of the serve return and court positioning are discussed in Chapter 5. Here follows a brief discussion of the mechanics of returning the serve and the resultant spins that can be used. The serve return motion is relatively short—somewhere between a high volley and a regular forehand or backhand. To help keep your backswing short, remember two things. First, make a full pivot and get your weight onto the foot nearest the ball; this gets the racket back. Second, on the backhand, keep the hitting elbow well away from your body (in front of it) during the pivot. On the forehand, keep the elbow close to the body.

A straight backswing is used to take the racket back for most serve returns. The racket goes back at about chest level rather than at waist level, since the ball will bounce higher than on a normal drive. This allows you to position the racket so you can still hit through the flight of a higher-bouncing ball. As you pivot, stay forward on your toes and lean a little forward with the front shoulder. This encourages you to transfer your weight forward into the shot as you hit. (Adjust your feet so you can step directly into the ball—avoid stepping across.) The ball must be met well in front of, and away from, the body.

The Drive Return

Meet the ball with the racket face beveled "flat," or perpendicular to the flight of the ball. Lift the ball up slightly as the racket moves forward. Finish with the racket face perpendicular to the flight of the ball.

To get more topspin, drop the racket head slightly below the ball on the backswing, and finish higher above the ball.

The Underspin Return

For the underspin return, open the racket face on the backswing and hit forward through the flight of the ball, keeping the racket face beveled open on the finish. As with a regular slice, finish with the wrist at eye level.

If you take a little pace off the ball and use a shorter swing, the underspin slice return becomes a "chip."

The Underspin Return

NET PLAY

Forehand Approach Volley

The Approach Volley

As you learn to hit harder and play more aggressively, you will come to the net more often. In many cases, such as when coming to net after your serve, you will have to hit a transition volley from midcourt before getting to your "home-base" position (10 to 15 feet from the net and slightly toward the court side to which the ball has been hit). The important thing to remember is to always be "set" when your opponent is contacting the ball so that you can change direction and react to the return. The simplest way to get set is just to jump to a "split" stop, landing on the balls of both feet at the instant your opponent contacts the ball.

"Read" the return, then while the ball is in the air, react by moving diagonally forward to it with a couple of quick steps, and then balance as you step into the volley. The diagram below shows footwork for the forehand volley.

The Forehand Approach Volley

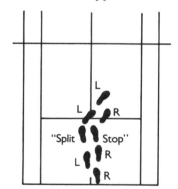

Usually this approach volley will be low at your feet. When the ball is low, you may want to open the racket face slightly on contact to put a little underspin on the ball and give it depth. Keep your wrist firm, meet the ball well in front of your body, and lift the racket forward into the flight of the ball with a short but smooth follow-through. If the ball is high, you can move in more quickly after getting "set." The racket may go back farther on the backswing, since you may turn more. Remember, since high volleys from midcourt are frequently hit into the net, hit out on the ball rather than down. The ball that is waist level or higher can be hit very flat.

Backhand Approach Volley

The Drop Volley

The Drop Volley

Once you are at the net, you may find occasions when you want to drop the volley very softly over the net—for instance, when your opponent is deep in the playing court and his or her return is dipping low to you. For the drop volley, open the racket face on contact and relax your wrist. Use very little follow-through. This takes the speed off the ball and makes it land short. However, as in the drop shot from the backcourt, remember that your opponent will probably win the point if he or she can actually get to the ball.

Returning Deeper Lobs

Any lobs landing near the service line should be hit flat or with little spin. Footwork is extremely important to hitting a good overhead. Turn sideways, and move your feet quickly into position. (In effect, you should be able to reach up with your left hand and catch the ball high and in front of your body.) Try to "set" on your back foot so that as you hit you can transfer your weight onto the front foot.

As the lob goes deeper, however, you may want to put some spin on the overhead so as to give it more control and, in essence, play it almost like an approach shot. This will help give you time to get back into position at the net for the put-away on the next shot. If the ball goes behind you, the most effective way to transfer your weight and hitting shoulder into the shot is to use a scissors kick in midair, thrusting the right foot forward as you hit (see photos of "The Deep Overhead").

The Deep Overhead

Playing the Game

Now that you have an understanding of the strokes of tennis and feel comfortable with at least the basic ones, you are ready to begin playing the game.

As an introduction to tennis strategy, the basic rules, scoring, and etiquette of tennis will be reviewed.

THE RULES OF TENNIS

Server and Receiver

The players (or teams) stand on opposite sides of the net. The player who first delivers the ball is called the *server;* and the other player is the *receiver.*

Choice of Service or Side

The choice of side (that is, who plays on which side of the net) for the first game and the right to be server or receiver in the first game are decided by toss. Generally one player spins a racket and the other player calls one of the options presented by the markings on the racket ("upside-down" or "right-side-up," "M" or "W," "number" or "no number," and so on). The player winning the toss may choose or require the opponent to choose—for the first game—either the right to be server or receiver (in which case the other player chooses the side of the net) or the side of the net (in which case the other player chooses the right to be server or receiver).

The service is delivered alternately from the right and left courts, beginning from the right court, and is directed into the diagonally opposite service court. At the conclusion of each game, the server becomes the receiver and the receiver becomes the server. Players change sides after each odd-numbered game in a set—that is, after the first game, the third game, the fifth game, and so on.

Faults

A player has two attempts to get the serve in play. If either of these attempts is not good, it is deemed a *fault.* Examples of faults are:

1. The server fails to hit the ball into the proper court.
2. The server misses the ball in attempting to strike it. (It may be tossed several times without penalty.)
3. The ball served touches a permanent fixture (other than the net) or the server's partner before it hits the ground.
4. A foot fault is committed.

A *foot fault* is called if:

1. The server touches the baseline or the court area within the baseline before hitting the ball.
2. The server changes position by walking or running before hitting the ball. (A server may jump at the serve, and one or both feet may be over the baseline, provided the server touches the playing court or line only *after* hitting the ball.)
3. The server serves from outside the area between the sideline and the center mark.

Lets

A *let* is a ball in play that touches the net, strap, or band and is otherwise good. When a let occurs on a service, the serve is replayed. When a let occurs during any other play, play continues uninterrupted.

A let is called when play is interrupted by such things as a ball rolling onto the court or a ball actually breaking during a point, or if the serve is delivered before the receiver is ready and the receiver has made no attempt to return that serve.

When a Player Loses the Point

A player loses the point if:

1. The player serves a double fault.
2. The player fails to return the ball before it bounces twice (the ball may be hit before it bounces, except on the return of serve, or after it bounces once only), or the player does not return the ball into the opponent's court.
3. The player returns the ball so that it hits the ground, a permanent fixture (fence, umpire's stand), or another object that lies outside the lines that bound the opponent's court.
4. The player volleys the ball and fails to make a good return even when standing outside the court.
5. The player *deliberately* touches the ball in play with the racket more than once when making a stroke (a "double hit") or *deliberately* "carries" the ball. (If *not* deliberate, a "double hit" and a "carry" are both legal and the ball is left in play.) In doubles, the ball may be returned by only one partner.
6. The player touches the net or the ground within the opponent's court with the racket or anything the player is wearing or carrying.
7. The player volleys the ball before it has passed the net.
8. The ball in play in any way touches the player or anything the player wears or carries *except* the racket.
9. The player throws the racket at and hits the ball.
10. The player deliberately commits any act that hinders the opponent in making a stroke.

Identifying a Good Return

A return is good if:

1. The ball lands on the line.
2. The ball touches the net, provided it passes over and lands in the proper court.
3. The player reaches over the net to hit a ball that, of its own accord, has blown or rebounded back to the other side, provided the player does not touch the net with racket, body, or clothing.

4. The player's racket passes over the net after the ball has been returned, provided the net is not touched.

5. The player returns a ball that has hit another ball already lying in the court. (A player may request a ball lying in the opponent's court to be removed, but not while the ball is in play.)

6. The ball is returned outside the post, provided it lands in the proper court.

7. A player cannot call a ball out when there is no official and each player is making the calls on his or her own side of the net.

Order of Service in Doubles

In doubles, the order of serving is decided at the beginning of each set. The pair to serve in the first game of each set decide which partner shall do so. The other partner serves the third game. The opposing pair decide which partner shall serve the second game of the set. The other partner then serves the fourth game. This order is followed throughout the set so that each player serves every fourth game.

If a player serves out of turn, the correct player must serve as soon as the mistake is discovered. All points earned are counted. If a complete game is played with the wrong player serving, the order of serve remains as altered.

Order of Receiving in Doubles

In doubles, the order for receiving is determined at the beginning of each set. The receiving pair decide who is to receive the first point, and that player continues to receive the serves directed to that particular service court throughout the set. (This also means that that player receives every other point in every other game.) The other partner does the same to the serves directed to the other service court.

If a player receives out of turn, he or she remains in that position until the completion of the game in which it is discovered. The partners then resume their original positions.

THE SCORING OF TENNIS

The Scoring of a Game

First Point: When a player (or team) wins his or her (or their) first point, the score for that player (or team) is called "15."

Second Point: When a player (or team) wins his or her (or their) second point, the score for that player (or team) is called "30."

Third Point: When a player (or team) wins his or her (or their) third point, the score for that player (or team) is called "40."

Fourth Point: When a player (or team) wins his or her (or their) fourth point, the score for that player (or team) is called "game," unless both players (or teams) have won three points, in which case the score is called "deuce."

After Deuce: When the score is "deuce," one player (or team) must win two consecutive points to win the game. The first point after deuce is called "advantage." If the *server* wins the first point after deuce, the score is called "advantage (ad) in." If the *receiver* wins the first point after deuce, the score is called "advantage (ad) out."

To help keep track of the correct score, the server should state the score just before serving each point. The server's score is *always* given first. For example, if the server has won two points and the receiver one, the server announces the score as "30-15." To avoid confusion, remember that if the total number of points played is an *even* number, then the ball is to be served from the *right* side of the court; if the total number of points played is an *odd* number, then the ball is to be served from the left side of the court.

No-Ad Scoring. A "sudden death" method of scoring can be substituted for the standard game scoring described above. This "no-ad" method is popular in many events, particularly school matches, since it cuts down the total playing time. Points are scored 1, 2, 3, 4, and the first player or team to score 4 points wins the game. There is no deuce. In singles or doubles, if the score reaches 3-3 the receiver chooses the service court from which to receive. In mixed doubles, if a woman serves the seventh point, the woman on the other team receives; if a man serves, the other man receives.

Server has won:	Receiver has won:	Score is:
1 point	0 point	15-love
2	0	30-love
3	0	40-love
4	0	game
3	1	40-15
3	2	40-30
1	1	15-all
2	2	30-all
3	3	deuce
4	3	ad in
3	4	ad out
5	3	game (server)

The Scoring of a Set

Conventionally, the player or team first winning six games wins the set, provided the player or team is ahead by at least two games. (If the score is 5-5 (5-all), play continues until one side gets two games ahead—7-5, 8-6, etc.) An average set takes about 30 minutes to complete.

Tie-Break Scoring. Tie-break scoring may be used in any event once the score in any set reaches six games all. The following system is used in the "12 point" tie-break scoring:

Singles. The player who first wins seven points wins the game and the set, provided the lead is by a margin of at least two points. If the score reaches six points all, the game is extended until a two-point lead is achieved. Numerical scoring (1, 2, 3, 4, 5, etc.) is used throughout the tie-break game.

The player whose turn it is to serve is the server for the first point. The opponent is the server for the second and third points. Thereafter, each player serves alternately for two consecutive points until the game and set have been won.

From the first point, each service is delivered alternately from the right and left courts, beginning from the right court. If service from a wrong side of the court goes undetected, all play resulting from such wrong service or services stands, but the inaccuracy of station must be corrected immediately after it is discovered.

Players change ends after every six points and at the conclusion of the tie-break game, at which time the final set score is called "7-6."

The tie-break game counts as one game for the ball change, except that, if the balls are due to be changed at the beginning of the tie-break, the change is delayed until the second game of the following set.

Doubles. The procedure for singles applies in doubles as well. The player whose turn it is to serve is the server for the first point. Thereafter, each player serves in rotation for two points, in the same order as previously in that set, until the winners of the game and set have been decided.

Rotation of service. The player (or pair in the case of doubles) who served first in the tie-break game receives service in the first game of the following set.

The Scoring of a Match

A match is completed when one person or side wins two of three sets. In top men's tournaments, however, a match often consists of three of five sets. A 10-minute break is mandatory if requested by either player or side between the third and fourth sets and is mandatory between the second and third sets for all youth events (16 years and under), although optional for boys of 16 or under.

The Point Penalty System

Use of the U.S. Tennis Association (U.S.T.A.) Point Penalty System is mandatory in any sanctioned tournament at district or sectional championship level or above. In other tournaments its use is at the discretion of the referee, who—before the start of the tournament or of any round or any match—may order its use. The purposes of the system are: (1) to ensure continuous play, (2) to deter unsportsmanlike conduct, and (3) to ensure on-time appearance for matches.

1. The following rule violations relate to continuous play and result in point penalties:
   a. A player or team takes more than 30 seconds between points.
   b. A player or team takes more than 90 seconds to change sides.
   c. A player or team takes more than 3 minutes to resume play after an injury.
   d. A player prolongs an argument longer than 30 seconds after having been directed to resume play. (If any time violation has been penalized, the passage of an additional 30 seconds is the basis for any additional penalty.)

2. The following code violations relate to unsportsmanlike conduct and result in point penalties:
   a. Visible or audible profanity or obscenity.
   b. Abuse (throwing or slamming) of racket, balls, or equipment.
   c. Verbal or physical abuse of a player or official.

3. If a player or team fails to appear on time for a match, that player or team may be penalized as follows:
   a. Less than five minutes late—loss of service/end option, plus one game.
   b. Five to 10 minutes late—loss of service/end option, plus two games.
   c. Ten to 15 minutes late—loss of service/end option, plus three games.
   d. More than 15 minutes late—default.

The point penalties are assigned as follows:

First offense—a warning

Second offense—one point

Third offense—one game

Fourth offense—default

THE ETIQUETTE OF TENNIS

Spectator Conduct

Whether you are a casual spectator watching an informal match or a member of a large crowd watching a championship tournament, you should be aware of some "unwritten rules." Player concentration is essential to top performance, and anything that detracts from concentration could affect the outcome of an entire match. The general rule is The Golden Rule—govern your actions as you would have others act if you were playing. Here are some specific rules:

1. Remain seated in the areas provided for spectators. Never sit on any benches or seats within the fenced area unless you have a specific function.
2. Keep quiet. Nothing is more disturbing than unnecessary conversation.
3. Applaud good play only *after* the point is completed.
4. If you are interested in the score, then keep score yourself. Do not continually bother the players by asking the score.
5. If you disagree with a decision, keep your opinion to yourself.
6. Referee a match only if acting in official capacity. (If you are asked to serve as umpire or linesman, you should do so willingly.)
7. If you are heading for another court, walk inconspicuously behind the fence of the court at the conclusion of the point.

Player Conduct

Good sportsmanship is the key to tennis etiquette. Treat others as you desire to be treated. Here are some specific rules that will make tennis more enjoyable for you and for those around you:

1. Know your opponent. Before you play, greet your opponent and introduce yourself.
2. Spin your racket to decide the choice of serve and side *before* you walk onto the court.
3. After a brief warmup (10 minutes maximum), ask whether your opponent wishes to practice any serves. All practice serves should be taken by both players *before* any points are played. Never agree to merely take the "first one in."
4. Begin a point as a server only if you have two balls in your hand or on your person.
5. Don't serve until your opponent is ready.
6. Never fail to observe the foot-fault rule. This is considered a breach of tennis etiquette.
7. Keep score accurately and, when serving, periodically announce the score.
8. Return only balls that are good, especially on the serve.
9. Call the balls on your side of the net (say "out" if the ball is out), and trust your opponent to do the same. Call faults and lets loud and clear. If the ball is in, or if you are unsure, you must play the ball as good and say nothing.
10. Talk only when pertinent to the match, and then only when the ball is not in play. However, acknowledge a good play by your partner or opponent.
11. Control your emotions and temper.
12. After each point, collect all balls on your side of the net and return them directly to the server. Don't lean on the net to retrieve a ball—the net cables break easily.

13. When the match is completed, leave no balls or debris on the court.

14. Retrieve balls from an adjacent court by waiting until the point is over and then do so politely by saying "Thank you" or "Ball, please."

15. Return balls from an adjacent court by waiting until play in progress has been completed and then tossing or rolling them to the nearest player.

16. Call a "let" when there is reasonable interference during play (such as another ball entering your court).

17. Make no excuses. At the conclusion of play, shake hands with and thank your opponent for the match. Congratulate your opponent if he or she has won.

18. If others are waiting, don't monopolize the courts. Either play doubles or rotate at the conclusion of each set.

19. Always dress properly—be neat and wear a shirt.

Tournament Conduct

It is a privilege to have your entry accepted into a tournament. Here are some ways to show your gratitude.

1. Report to the tournament desk at least 15 minutes ahead of the scheduled time. If you cannot, let the tournament desk know ahead of time that you may be late or must default.

2. As the winner, return all balls to the tournament desk, report the score, and ascertain your next playing time.

3. Offer to help the tournament committee (with calling lines, preparing courts, transportation, etc.).

4. Thank the tournament director at the end of the tourney. If room and board were provided, adequately thank those responsible.

Playing the Game: Singles Strategy

The player with sound strokes is at a distinct advantage in a tennis match. Still, it is essential to realize that strokes are only a means to an end. Strokes enable you to make the best use of strategy, and once you have learned them you must try to use them as intelligently and efficiently as possible.

The discussion of strategy begins by emphasizing elements of concentration. This is followed by a description of the uses of the serve and serve return. Considerations for the backcourt rally are outlined, such as the importance of keeping the ball in play and hitting deep, when to hit cross court or down the line, and when to hit short. Then the discussion moves to the components of a more offensive game: how to approach the net on groundstrokes and serve. Finally, the principles of defense against the net rusher are presented.

ELEMENTS OF CONCENTRATION

There is a great advantage to good concentration—to playing each point. Point-by-point play puts tremendous pressure on your opponent. In fact, it is possible to lose more points than you win and still win the set. Know the critical points. All points are important, but on certain points it is critical to avoid needless mistakes. At other times, you can be more aggressive and take some chances.

Play ahead. There is tremendous pressure on your opponent if you are ahead. Since the deuce-court points are the ones that usually put you ahead or cause you to fall behind, concentrate on getting the jump on your opponent by not being careless in the deuce court. Play steadier in the deuce court. Get ahead with the first point and work hard on the third point—this can keep you from falling behind, or it can give you a commanding lead.

As the game nears a climax, apply all the concentration possible on every ball that is hit. On advantage points like 40-30, don't gamble too much on your serve, since the server generally has the advantage. If returning, however, be aggressive.

Winning the long rallies is a sign of match toughness and gives you a tremendous psychological advantage. Above all, don't make a careless mistake that might end a long rally.

The first games in every set are important. Be ready to begin play. Don't make the mistake of "overhitting" early in the match until you find out whether or not your opponent can hurt you. (This is a common mistake when people are playing someone they think is better.)

As the set goes along, if you haven't had many chances, when you finally get one, be aggressive and go for it! Don't let an opportunity pass by. The seventh game in each set is critical; often the winner of the seventh game will win the set.

THE USE OF THE SERVE

As a beginner, you were probably primarily concerned with just getting the ball into play and maybe to your opponent's backhand. As you gain more confidence you can use more variety on your serve (speed, spin, and placement) and start to use the serve to offensive advantage.

The Importance of the First Serve

Your strategy as a server should be to get at least two-thirds of your first serves in the court. Don't waste your first serve just because you are entitled to another. Although it is true that you can serve more aggressively (and yet competitively) on the first serve because you have another chance, remember, if you miss that first serve, you are like a baseball pitcher falling behind the batter. There is much less opportunity to take the offensive. The receiver knows this and will play accordingly, especially since your opponent then expects the second serve to go to the backhand.

On critical points, however, when it is important to keep the pressure on your opponent, a much higher percentage of first serves *must* be good, even if it means serving less aggressively. If you are substantially behind, you might as well serve more aggressively and try to get back in the game quickly.

Unless you are trying to serve at an extreme angle, depth is important, especially on a second serve. If the serve lands short, the receiver has many more options and can play much more aggressively, as described in the section on serve return.

Above all, don't double fault. Doing so is analogous to the baseball pitcher walking the batter. A double fault at "ad out" is just like a pitcher walking in a run.

Mix Up Serves

A hard, flat serve to the backhand may be your most effective serve, but you cannot use it all the time, any more than a pitcher would use only a fast ball. Keep your opponent guessing and off balance.

Serve *wide* to your opponent if:

1. You have a natural angle, such as a slice to the forehand in the forehand court or a twist to the backhand in the backhand court.

2. Your opponent undercuts (slices) most returns. This may mean your opponent cannot return well with the drive, the natural return for a wide ball, especially when hitting cross court.

3. Your opponent assumes a faulty "set" position—too far behind the baseline or too close to the center of the court.

4. Your opponent generally backs up or runs wide to return a wide serve instead of stepping in and cutting off the angle.

5. There is a letdown in concentration (after a long point or a long game). This is a good time for a wide serve to the forehand.

6. Your opponent moves in close for the return, in an attempt to come directly to the net. A wide serve pulls your opponent off the court, making it more difficult to get to the net.

The Use of Wide Serves

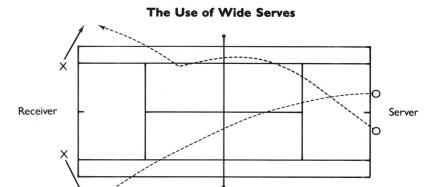

Serve in *tight* to your opponent (for example, to the forehand in the ad court) if:

1. Your opponent normally takes a big swing at the return. A ball close to the body makes a big swing difficult.

2. You are in trouble, such as 30-40 and serving a second serve. A tight serve not only cramps the return swing, but it cuts down the chance for an outright winner with an angled return. Don't give your opponent the angle on an important point.

Serve Down the Middle to Avoid Angled Return

Serve *high* to your opponent (topspins or twists) if:

1. Your opponent cannot return a high ball well. Many players cannot hit well through a high ball.

2. Your opponent moves backward to hit the return.

Vary the Speed

If you are serving hard and your opponent is returning well, realize that some receivers rely on the speed of the hard serve for the effectiveness of their return. Don't hesitate to use more spin occasionally to slow the ball down, even on a first serve.

If you want to serve hard, remember that the net is lowest in the center and the ball gets to the receiver sooner down the middle than when it is served wide. Also, although such a return ball may be coming back faster, your opponent has less angle for the return.

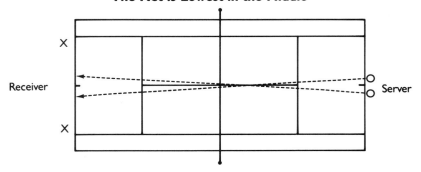

The Net is Lowest in the Middle

THE USE OF THE SERVE RETURN

A good serve gives an initial advantage, whether or not the server comes to the net after the serve. However, a good return can at least neutralize the advantage. In practicing receiving, work first to develop a consistent serve return and then to develop a return that can turn the point into an advantage for you.

Positioning

When waiting for the serve, assume a "set" position slightly behind the baseline that bisects the angle to which the serve may be hit. If you have to move to the side to hit the return, then move *diagonally forward* to cut down the angle. Don't let a wide serve drive you back. Likewise, don't charge the ball. A common beginner's mistake is to run forward unnecessarily instead of turning. Stay forward and down on the return, letting your front knee bend some.

Move Diagonally Forward to Return Wide Serves

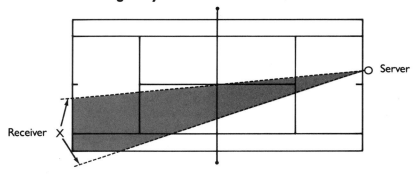

Vary the Return

Even though the basic return is usually a rather flat drive, vary your returns. Stand back a little farther sometimes, take a bigger swing, and drive the return with more topspin. (Against a net rusher, this can upset the serve and volley rhythm, since the server must now take a couple of extra steps to get in to the ball.) Or, move in closer in order to hit the ball sooner (especially when your opponent has had difficulty serving and has been serving short), even to the point of occasionally going to net behind the return. Remember, the earlier you take the ball, the shorter the swing and the more underspin you'll put on the ball (which on serve returns means you will be using a slice or a chip).

Be Aggressive

Most of all, be positive. Look at returning serve as a challenge. Don't look up to return until you are really concentrating and mentally ready. (Sometimes, a deep breath at this stage helps.) Be on your toes; take a little jump up into the air just before the serve is hit, to help you get ready. Don't just stand in a batter's box and wait motionless for the pitch. Make the server know you are there. Move around. Make your opponent think of serving down the middle by standing wider in the court. Stand in close to make the server try to hit too good a second serve. Force the server to change serving rhythm by standing far back.

Make the server pay the price when a first serve is missed. It is reasonable to assume that the second serve will be to your backhand, and because the server is hitting it with more spin, it may be short as well. Be ready to move in and "chip and charge" into the net on the return, or—especially in the deuce court—when the server tosses the ball up, move to your left and "crank" a forehand return down the line.

Have a Plan

Before the ball is served, decide where you will return it and what kind of return to hit. Don't wait to see what kind of a serve it is and then react to it. Know ahead of time whether you will hit softly cross court to your opponent's backhand volley or whether you will hit hard down the line to your opponent's forehand.

Keep the pressure on the server in general by getting a high percentage of returns into play. But don't be afraid to "go for it" by hitting harder or closer to the line. (You can gamble more when you are returning serve, since the server usually has the advantage anyway. Remember, you only need to put together a couple of good shots to have a real chance to break serve.) When you get to "break point," be aggressive and "go for it," since you may not get other chances.

BACKCOURT TENNIS

Court Position

You must know where to wait for your opponent's shot in order to best be able to return it.

Bisect the Potential Angle of Return. Wait behind the baseline in a position that bisects the potential angle of your opponent's hit. For example, if the ball is being hit from Point A, assume a "set" position at Point B, slightly to the right of the center mark.

Assume Position to Bisect Return Angle

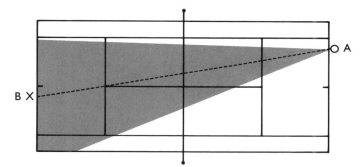

Stay Out of "No-Man's-Land." Be careful not to get caught in "no-man's-land" (midcourt) unless you are purposely going to the net. Balls will bounce behind you or at your feet if you are in the midcourt. These are difficult shots to return, and you will usually be forced to hit them up (defensively). If you have to run into no-man's-land for a short ball, return quickly to your home base 1 or 2 feet behind the baseline or go on to the net. Don't remain in no-man's-land.

"No-Man's Land"

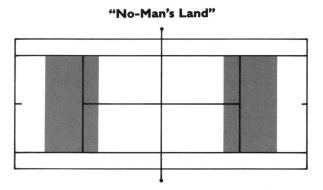

Keep the Ball in Play

Make Your Opponent Hit the Ball. This is the first and foremost rule in tennis, for the advanced player as well as the beginner. Concentrate on keeping the ball going back to your opponent. Don't let your opponent off the hook by trying an unnecessary shot, missing, or getting caught out of position.

Out-Rally Your Opponent. You need only hit the ball in the court one more time than your opponent to win the point. If you can keep the ball in play, you can pressure your opponent to hit a placement to beat you.

Play Percentage Tennis

Try to balance your errors and placements. Unnecessary errors—balls that could have been returned—account for 75 percent of all points lost. Only 25 percent, on the other hand, are lost because of placements—shots hit so well they could not have been returned. Three-quarters of the unnecessary errors are because the ball hits the net, and only one-quarter are because the ball lands out of bounds.

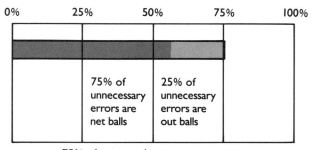

75% of points end in unnecessary error

Inevitably, you will make errors. Even in championship tennis there is rarely a perfect balance of errors and placements. But play percentage tennis and cut down on unnecessary errors. The player who wins is the one who makes fewer errors, especially at critical times.

Never try to hit the ball better than you have to in order to win the point. In a nutshell, this strategy separates the players who win from those who don't. It is this difference that makes some players better competitors than others.

Keep the Ball Deep

As you play more and encounter better players, you will find that merely keeping the ball in play is not enough. You must also keep the ball deep so as to prevent your opponent from reaching an offensive position at the net. A shot is considered deep if it lands within a couple of feet of the baseline.

Deep-Shot Area

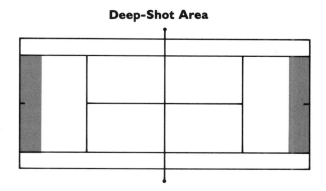

A deep shot makes it more difficult for your opponent to respond aggressively because the hitting angle is reduced, which means you have less court to cover.

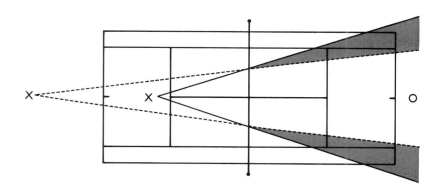

The ball should be returned high and deep (a "floater") whenever you are in trouble or out of position. This will give you time to recover into proper "set" position.

For the beginner who has not yet learned to hit the ball safely and with power, a deep ball must clear the net by a good 5 to 8 feet if it is hit from near the baseline. A beginner who hits from a greater distance behind the baseline may even have to hit a lob—a ball that clears the net by more than 10 feet—to keep the shot deep.

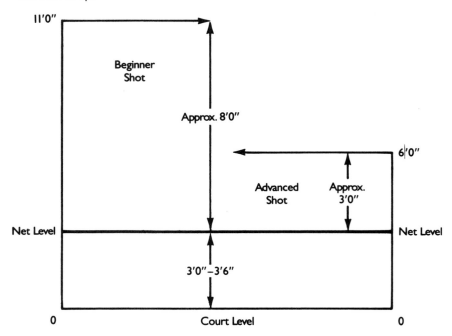

The deep, floater ball bounces higher and forces a beginning or intermediate opponent to move substantially back from the baseline to return the ball. (A more advanced player who hits with more power must clear the net by only 2 or 3 feet on most shots from the baseline.) In general, the farther behind the baseline any player is, the higher the ball must be hit to keep it deep.

Change the Pace of the Ball

The outcome of a backcourt rally can often be affected by the player who can change the pace (speed) of the ball effectively—either by changing spins or by using more or less power. The mix of powerful shots with some off-speed "float-ers" or solid underspins makes it difficult for your opponent to maintain a hitting rhythm. It therefore can decrease your opponent's ability to control the return to you, especially in terms of depth.

When to Hit Cross Court

Keeping the ball in play and keeping the ball deep are essential and primary strategies, but they are basically defensive. While thinking defensively and in terms of not making needless errors, you must also be thinking of ways to move your opponent from side to side or up and back. You can either return the ball diagonally across the net (cross court) or parallel to the side line (down the line). There are special considerations for both of these shots.

The cross-court shot, which is almost always a topspin drive, fits well into the strategy set forth so far. It is a *safe* shot for several reasons: (1) The cross-court shot gives you more margin when playing on a fast surface or in the wind (a down-the-line return of a cross-court shot will tend to ricochet wide off your racket). (2) Keeping the ball deep becomes less essential. Since a cross-court shot often has sufficient angle to pull your opponent wide, it is more difficult for him or her to get into a position to attack, even if the ball is short. (3) The ball must travel over the center of the net, which is 6 inches lower than at the sides. (4) The court is almost 5 feet longer diagonally—from one extreme corner to the other—than it is down the line.

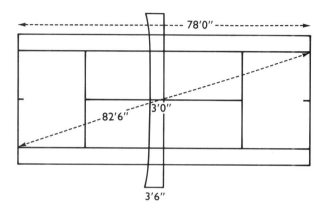

Use a cross-court shot:

1. *To get your opponent moving:* Start the point immediately with a cross-court shot. It makes your opponent run more since it can be hit to greater angles. The more your opponent has to run for a ball, the less chance he or she has to get set and therefore to transfer weight into a shot. This increases the chance of a weak return. Even if you are hitting to a strength, a cross-court shot will help to expose a weakness on the next shot.

2. *If your opponent hits down the line to you:* He or she will now have to move a considerable distance to get to your cross-court return. If you can return the down-the-line shot with an aggressive cross-court, it gives you an excellent chance to win the point outright.

3. *When you are out of position:* In this situation, you won't have so far to recover in order to be in position to bisect the potential angle of your opponent's return.

Cross-Court Return

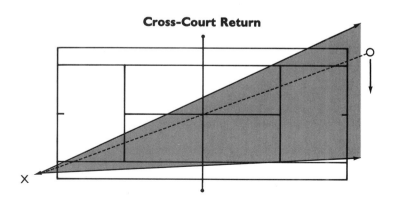

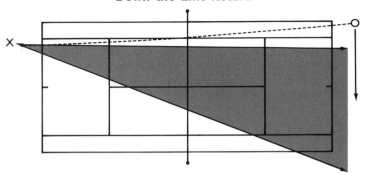

Down-the-Line Return

When to Hit Down the Line

Use a down-the-line shot:

1. As a change of routine to the basic cross-court pattern.

2. To hit to a player's weakness.

3. To hit behind a person running fast to cover the opposite side of the court.

4. As the basic attack shot to get to the net. (Usually you hit this ball early, since you want to get to the net as quickly as possible.)

Because the ball travels a shorter distance and over a higher part of the net than in a cross-court shot, and also because it is more difficult to follow through the flight of the ball, which means the ball tends to slide off the racket to the side, allow more margin for error on the down-the-line shot. Use considerable spin and aim well inside the line.

When to Hit Short

Basically you want to keep your opponent as far in the backcourt as possible. However, many players don't move forward as well as they move to the side. Also, some players stay in the backcourt because they feel insecure at net. If your opponent never moves up to the net, try returning the ball short to force your opponent to come to the net. Once your opponent gets to the net, try lobbing, for your opponent may be avoiding the net because of an overhead weakness.

You may also want to return short if your opponent is pulling you to the net and then successfully lobbing over you or passing you. If you are not effective when inadvertently pulled to the net, bring your opponent to the net instead by using a soft, short ball instead of an approach shot. Also, short shots following high floaters can be effective change-of-pace shots.

The extreme short ball, called a "drop shot," is hit with considerable underspin. It is usually used when the player thinks it will produce an outright winner. It should rarely be attempted, except when hitting from midcourt, for if your opponent can get to it, it will likely result in a put-away.

OFFENSIVE TENNIS

Approaching the Net on a Groundstroke

Backcourt tennis is primarily defensive tennis. The discussion has shown how basically defensive maneuvers (deep balls, or balls that move your opponent) can force weak or inaccurate returns.

During a backcourt rally you might hit aggressively and record your share of outright winners. However, better players generally use a backcourt rally primarily to set up a chance to attack at the net. (Beyond the beginning levels, there is a much higher percentage of winning shots or forced errors hit by the attacker at the net than when both players stay in the backcourt.)

When to Approach the Net. When a short ball (weak shot) is hit to you and you must move into midcourt to return it, you can:

1. Play it 100 percent defensively by returning it fairly softly, high, deep, and down the middle—giving your opponent no angle for return and giving yourself time to retreat to a more comfortable position behind the baseline.

2. Play it as a drop shot, which tends to pull your opponent up out of position.

3. Play it 100 percent offensively by approaching the net. Even intermediate players can have reasonable success playing at the net (we have seen how mechanically simple the volley really is), provided they come to net at the right time with the right shot. This correctly implies that the most critical factor in successful net play is the method used to get there—the approach shot itself.

Anticipation is a learned response. The more you play, the more you learn to "feel" the kind of return your opponent may hit. Anticipation of the short ball helps make your approach shot easier. You must learn to "feel" when the return may be short (the result of a deep, or hard, shot, or because the opponent had to run a great distance), and be mentally prepared to move in quickly. Anticipation will get you started a split second sooner and will allow you time to get to the ball and be balanced and set.

Think of getting to the net more often if:

1. The court is fast. This means your opponent will have less time to prepare to return your approach shot.

2. The wind is at your back. This gives your shot added speed and also hurries your opponent.

3. You feel your presence at the net may "pressure" your opponent into an error.

How to Approach the Net. When the return is weak, your thoughts should immediately change from steadier play to "attack." At the same time, don't get careless when you finally get the opportunity to attack. Remember, you have worked the entire rally to get the opportunity to come to the net. Don't overhit. Don't rush. Be content to use the approach shot as an interim shot to set up the winning volley (unless you have an obvious opening).

Try to hit the ball early on the approach. Contact the ball no later than at the top of its bounce. This gets you closer to the net, and it gives your opponent less time to prepare for the return. It is an axiom that: "The earlier a ball is met and the closer to the net you are, the shorter your swing need be." Most balls taken "on the rise" are hit with underspin, because the underspin shot requires less backswing and is easier to "time" with the shorter swing. In addition, the underspin ball tends to bounce low and even skid, which forces your opponent to hit up.

Court Position. Follow the ball to the net. In other words, if you hit the approach shot down the line, go to net a little off center (toward the near sideline). This will help you bisect the potential angle of return and thus best enable you to cover the shot.

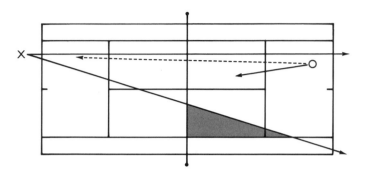

"Split" to a balanced stop. Hop up so that you land momentarily with both feet split apart on the court as your opponent contacts the ball. You then will be able to react efficiently when you see where the return is hit.

Come to net only when you feel you can get in close enough, commensurate with being completely "set" (usually about 15 feet from the net). This cuts down the potential angles of return (which are greater when you are farther from the net) but still alllows you to protect against a lob.

Where to Hit the Approach Shot. *Depth* is critical to an effective approach shot, for it substantially limits the angle available on the return. This is important, since a player cannot cover the entire width of the court. The deeper the approach shot, the more difficult it is to return the ball successfully cross court. There is less available angle to which to hit the passing shot, and it is mechanically more difficult to get the racket around the ball quickly enough to return cross court.

Thus, if the approach shot is hit deep, the net player can assume a "set" position closer to the sideline to which the ball is hit. By taking a step diagonally forward toward the near sideline, the net player should be able to cover any ball returned down the line. By taking a step diagonally toward the center of the court, the net player can cover most any ball returned cross court. The deeper the approach shot, the more the net rusher should expect a lob and thus does not get so close to the net.

Down the line is usually the best place to hit the approach shot. The net player assumes a position, about 15 feet from the net, that bisects the potential angle of return. If the approach shot is hit deep and down the line, the net player need stay only on that respective side of the court when going to the net. If, however, the approach shot is cross court, the net player has to move all the way across the center of the court to bisect the potential angle of return. There usually is not enough time to take the extra steps required to move across the court and still be set before the opponent returns.

A *cross-court* approach shot might be used if your opponent has a definite weakness on that side, or if the net rusher feels a winner may be hit on the down-the-line approach.

A *down-the-middle* approach shot might be used (1) if the opponent has very good angle returns (since it diminishes the angles), (2) if the opponent moves very fast (it cuts down any natural speed advantage, since the opponent has no place to run), and (3) to increase the chance of a lob return (since there is little angle to which to hit the passing shot).

Reacting to the Return Once at the Net. Footwork is important. After "splitting" to a stop at the instant your opponent contacts the ball, take several quick, small steps forward and "set" again to hit your volley. Avoid large or lunging steps. If the ball is one large step away, take three small, quick steps to reach it so you can be balanced when you hit the volley.

In general, you should volley to the open side of the court. (If the opponent's return is hit down the line, volley cross court; if the return is cross court, volley down the line.) The premise is that your opponent will have to hit the passing shot on the run, which may decrease the chance of an effective return. However, the net player must be certain to move across the center of the court after the volley in order to protect the court from a return down the line. As with an approach shot, if your opponent moves very fast and is also effective with angle returns, then you might want to play more volleys down the middle of the court, or even hit some behind the player. For example, if the opponent returns down the line, volley down the line; if the return is cross court, volley cross court.

If the ball is low, the volley must be deep or very sharply angled. Take the low ball as early as possible so it doesn't have time to drop far below the level of the net.

If the ball is lobbed very high, or if sun and wind are a deterrent, let the ball bounce before hitting your overhead. Otherwise, always hit it before it bounces. Hit the overhead aggressively from the forecourt (it is the most offensive shot in tennis), but play it with more spin when hitting from deeper in the backcourt.

Approaching the Net After Your Serve

Before you serve, make up your mind to either come to the net or stay back. Don't wait to see whether the serve is in or effective.

Consider coming to the net if:

1. You have a strong or effective serve. A forcing serve is more likely to elicit a weak and playable return.

2. You have a strong volley and overhead. An advanced player regularly may come to net behind both the first and second serves. An intermediate player will occasionally come to net behind the first serve and rarely behind the second. A beginner rarely will come to net behind either serve.

3. You are playing on a relatively fast surface, such as a fast hard court or grass court. A fast surface can make your serve more effective, whereas a rougher surface such as clay can slow down the bounce of the serve so much that the receiver has ample time to prepare for a good return.

4. You are serving with a strong wind at your back. This also gives the serve more pace and thus gives the receiver less time to prepare.

5. Your opponent is getting "grooved" into hitting one kind of return. If the receiver is not expecting you to come to net, the return ball will probably be kept deep by being hit fairly high above the net. This could give you a relatively easy volley. On the other hand, if you regularly have been coming to net behind your serve, the receiver will be trying to return the ball low, which would make it land short. If you stay back on your serve, you may have the opportunity to hit a forehand or backhand approach shot after this short return.

Coming to the Net Behind Your Serve. As the first step in getting to the net on the follow-through of the serve, bring your back foot across the baseline and into the court. Continue to move forward in the direction of the serve until your opponent contacts the ball. At that instant, you should be completely balanced and "set" by virtue of your "split" stop.

1. You should have time for three or four steps before coming to your "split" stop. This puts you in the vicinity of the service line, although behind it. You must accept the fact that, on your serve, it is impossible to get all the way to "home base" at the net from behind the baseline before the ball is returned. Thus, you will have to hit one volley or half volley from the difficult and relatively vulnerable no-man's-land.

2. Remember to follow the ball to the net and make the initial "split" stop on the side of the court to which the ball has been served, so that you can cover the down-the-line return.

3. After you "split" stop, move forward with several small, quick steps to where you want to contact the ball. "Set" again for the volley. This should allow you to contact the ball in front of the service line.

Hitting the Volley. If there is an opening, you probably will want to volley to it to force the receiver to hit the passing shot on the run. For example, a wide serve to the backhand in the backhand (ad) court leaves the forehand court open—especially if the ball is returned down the line. If there is no obvious opening, play the shot conservatively and deep. (In fact, many good players volley essentially down the middle of the court in order to cut down the angle for the passing shot.)

If the return is down the middle and low, you are not yet close enough to put any angle on your return, so the premium is on volleying deep. If the return is hit wide, you may be able to use more angle on your volley and therefore may not want so much depth.

After you have hit the first volley, follow the ball the rest of the way to the net, as you would when approaching on a groundstroke. (Remember, your "home base" is about 15 feet from the net toward the side of the court the ball is on.) Treat the first volley like an approach shot—don't overhit the ball. The first volley should set up your second volley.

Defending Against the Net Rusher

How to Return Serve Against the Net Rusher. The primary objective of the receiver is to return the serve low and at the net rusher's feet. This forces the net rusher to volley up. This is usually a less offensive volley, since the shot can't be hit as hard. You will have to decide what kind of return is most effective. Here are a few suggestions:

1. Against players who have a volley weakness on one side or the other, you may want to concentrate on returning to the forehand volley or to the backhand volley, as the case might be.

2. Against players who volley very well when pulled wide—especially those with a great deal of touch or who may be very quick—you may want to return more balls down the middle.

3. The basic return should be a solid, fairly flat, or topspin drive, although against net rushers who prefer to volley a hard return you may want to try some softer underspin or chip returns.

4. Try moving in when your opponent is getting too close to the net for the first volley. You can keep the net rusher from getting in so close if you take the ball sooner yourself. Perhaps you can beat such a player to the net by using the return of service as an approach shot.

5. Stand farther back than usual if you want more time to react. This also may upset the server's timing in coming in, since two or three more steps are needed before the volley. Keep the ball down the middle to minimize the chance for an angle volley, and be prepared to lob on the second shot.

6. Be aggressive when you get a chance to "break serve."

Above all, if you are unsuccessful in returning one way, change and try something different. Examples include standing in closer to or standing farther from the net, hitting harder or hitting softer, and hitting for more angle or hitting down the middle.

Once Your Opponent Is at the Net. Most important in defending against the attack is not to be pressed into trying too good a shot against the net rusher. Don't feel you have only one shot in which to win the point. The axiom is: "Make your opponent hit the ball to beat you." Your opponent does not win the point automatically merely by being at the net. It is remarkable how many "sure winners" are missed at the net. Unless you are confident of hitting an outright winner, use your first shot to pull your opponent out of position and open up the court, and then be more aggressive on the second shot. Take your time. Don't be rushed into not getting "set" or not staying down with the shot.

The Use of the Lob. Most players think only of trying to blast the ball past their opponent. Thus the lob is probably the most underused shot in tennis, yet it is one of the most effective. Give yourself plenty of margin (never miss a lob wide), and get the ball up high into the air. Any time you succeed in getting a lob over the net player's head, move into the net yourself. Even if the lob doesn't get over the net player's head, if it is deep it tends to push that player back away from the net and to open up the court in front of him or her for a passing shot.
Use the lob:

1. Whenever you are hitting from substantially behind the baseline.

2. If the sun is a factor, even if you are not deep in the court.

3. On windy days. Although it is difficult to lob in the wind, it is even more difficult to hit an overhead in the wind. (Don't lob as high on windy days, and remember that it is easier to lob when the wind is at your back.)

4. On hot days, particularly early in the match. If the match turns out to be a long one, conditioning could be a deciding factor, and continually returning lobs is tiring.

5. Often on balls that are volleyed down the middle, even when returning from near the baseline. (You don't have much angle for a passing shot.)

6. Occasionally on short balls. A surprise quick lob can be effective.

Adding topspin to a lob can be very effective, particularly if it is not an obvious lobbing situation or when lobbing against the wind.

The Use of Passing Shots. The most important principle in the use of passing shots is to keep the ball low so the volleyer who reaches the ball will be forced to hit it up, thus decreasing the opportunity to make an aggressive return shot. Topspin balls drop faster than flat or underspin balls. Therefore, most passing shots are hit with substantial topspin.

The most common passing drives are hit *down the line*. The ball gets to the opponent quickly down the line and affords little time to prepare. Also it is difficult for a player running to the side to get the racket around the ball fast enough to pass cross court. Since the net player is probably covering the down-the-line shot, you must hit the ball fairly hard to get it by. Try to stay forward with the ball as long as you can, and don't pull up from the ball with your body. After the shot, recover quickly, since the net player probably will try to volley to the cross-court opening.

The *cross-court* passing shot is a good one if you have the opportunity to hit it (for instance, when the ball is volleyed short). In general, use a lot of topspin when attempting a cross-court passing shot. If you keep your ball cross court, your opponent has less opening to volley to.

It is less essential to hit the ball hard when you attempt to pass cross court than when you pass down the line. If your shot is soft and low, there is little the volleyer can do. Try this soft change-of-pace shot occasionally to pull your opponent in to the net and out of position enough to set up the passing shot or quick lob on your next hit.

Playing the Game:
Doubles Strategy

INTRODUCTION TO BASIC DOUBLES

Doubles is a game of *position*. Each partner is primarily responsible for his or her own side of the court and should be able to cover any return the opponents hit, as long as he or she knows where to be in a particular situation. The discussion begins by describing each player's basic starting position and how that player moves from "home base" by adjusting his or her position to the most commonly occurring situations.

Serving and Receiving Positions

The *server* must stand behind the baseline, generally near the center of the service side of the court. This allows the server to be in position after the serve to get to any ball returned to that side of the court.

The *receiver* should assume a "home base" that bisects the angle to which the server may hit. (Usually this is about 1 foot from the alley, but it may vary somewhat depending on whether the serve is from close to the center or wide, by the alley.) The receiver should begin the match standing near the baseline. However, if the opponent regularly serves very hard, the receiver must move back a couple of feet. If the opponent often serves quite soft, such as on a second serve, the receiver can elect to stand a couple of feet inside the baseline. (If starting from inside the baseline, the receiver should either move back after the return, or—if the serve is very short—use the return as an approach shot and move up to the net with his or her partner.)

Net Player Positions When the Ball Is Served

The *server's partner* should start in a position at the net. The net player's "home base" position is approximately 10 feet from the net (halfway between the net and the service line) and 1 or 2 feet from the alley.

The *receiver's partner* should begin by standing on the middle of the service line on his or her side of the court. This is only a temporary position, for if the receiver's partner were to start at the normal "home base" and the receiver were to hit a bad return (that is, to the net player), there would be no way for him to cover the center of the court. If the return inadvertently goes to the opposing net player, the receiver's partner should try to cover the center of the court. If the return is good (that is, back to the server), the receiver's partner should move up to the net player's normal "home base" while the point continues.

The primary responsibility of the net player is to let no ball pass by on the alley side of the court and to force all balls to the middle. In addition, the net player should constantly be looking for the *poach*—that is, a ball that can be intercepted and cut off.

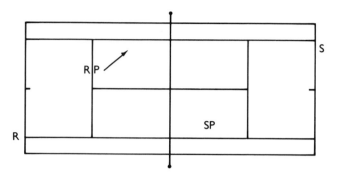

The Cross-Court Rally

Basic doubles play begins with the cross-court rally, since the server must direct the serve diagonally across the court to the receiver. The primary objective of the two *backcourt players* is to keep the ball away from the net players and thus to rally back and forth to each other. In addition, the backcourt players should try to keep the ball high enough over the net so that it lands deep in the opponent's court. The best way to do this is with a high, floating ball rather than with a "beeline" ball that barely skims the top of the net. After each shot, the backcourt player returns to "home base" about 1 or 2 feet behind the baseline, at a point that bisects the potential angle of the opponent's return.

The *net players* slide toward the side of the court to which the ball is returned by taking a side-skip or two in either direction from "home base." For example, in the diagram below, player A has returned the ball to player B. Net player C moves toward the alley to prevent player B's return ball from going down the alley. Net player D moves toward the center of the court in order to cover the middle in case partner B should inadvertently return the ball to net player C. The net players should watch the ball at all times except when their partner is serving.

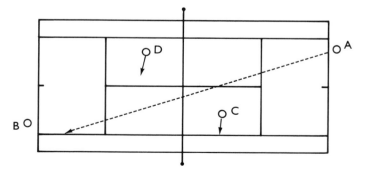

If a return goes short, the backcourt player moves into midcourt to return it but, rather than remaining in "no-man's-land" (the middle of the court, where most balls bounce), moves up and joins his or her partner at the net. The objective in doubles often is to get to the net with your partner when (1) there is extra angle to which to hit, since you are up close; (2) you can get the ball back to your opponents much sooner and thus give them less time to prepare; and (3) you can often hit down on the ball. Therefore, not only do the partners of the server and receiver start at the net, but the backcourt player joins his or her partner at the net whenever he or she can get there and be "set" by the time the opponent hits the ball. A short ball is the first of three examples of when to join your partner at the net. If you have to move well inside the playing court to return the ball, then you have to take only a couple of more steps to go all the way to the net.

When Both Partners Are at the Net

When both partners are at the net, such as when the backcourt player moves up to return a short ball, a new "home base" a little farther from the net must be assumed. This is because once both partners are at the net, each is responsible for every ball on his or her respective side of the court. Thus, the new "home base" is about 15 feet from the net (instead of about 10 feet). Although the net players have now sacrificed some volley angle, they can still move forward to hit the volley before it gets too low. Yet, by putting their rackets in the air and moving a couple of steps back, they should be able to use their overhead to hit any lobbed ball before it bounces.

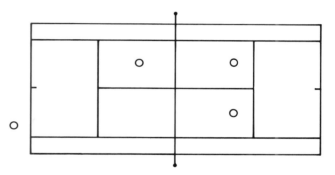

When both opponents (B and D) are at the net, the opposing net player (C) remains at the net in case his or her partner (A) is able to return the ball low. When this happens, player C should be ready to move in and cut the ball off (a "poach"), since the opposing net player (B or D) will be volleying up.

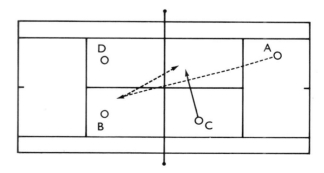

However, if player A lobs, then net player C retreats back toward the baseline, primarily in order not to get hurt by the opposing team's overhead smash, but also to have a little more time to react to the shot. Net player C is trying to get back all the way behind the baseline, but no matter where he or she is located when the opponent hits the ball, the net player should stop and "set" so as to have a chance to react. It is important to realize that the partner will most likely lob when both opponents are at the net, and the net player should be ready to move back at the instant his or her partner hits the lob, especially if the partner is returning from a position deep in the court. (One reason the net player always watches the ball except when his or her partner is serving is so that the lob can be recognized immediately and the net player will have time to move back.)

When both partners are at the net, the opponents should direct most drives down the middle so the net players are forced to volley with little angle. A lob may be hit to either partner to get that player away from the net and to open up some room in the forecourt for the next drive.

The Lob in Basic Doubles

The Short Lob. During the course of a cross-court rally, one of the backcourt players may attempt to hit a lob over the opposing net player's head. The lob is not always successful and may go short, giving the net player a chance to hit an overhead. When this happens, then:

1. The net player immediately says "mine" so partner knows that the net player is taking it.
2. To avoid being hit and to gain time to react, the lobber's partner moves back from the net as far as possible before the opponent hits the overhead.
3. Since the lobbed ball is high, it is in the air long enough to give the partner of the player hitting the overhead time to get to the net and be "set" before the overhead is returned. (Both net players must remember to adjust to their new "home base" farther back in the service squares.) The short lob is the second example of when a backcourt player has time to join his or her partner at the net.

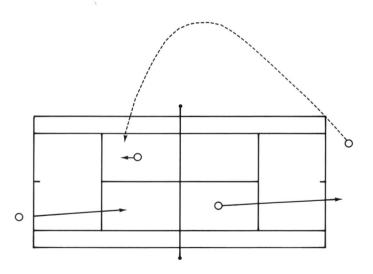

The Deep Lob. If the lob is hit as well as intended, it will get over the net player's head. When this happens, then:

1. The lobbing player can take advantage of what is usually thought of as a defensive shot by using the time the ball is in the air to join his or her partner at the net. This is the third example of when a backcourt player should come to the net. (Both net players must remember to adjust to their new "home base" farther back in the service squares.)

2. The player who is lobbed over, on seeing that the shot cannot be reached, yells "switch" to his or her partner. The net player then crosses over to the other side of the court to be able to cover the area the partner is leaving. The net player also moves diagonally back to behind the baseline, expecting the opponents to be able to hit an overhead.

3. The backcourt partner crosses over to the other side of the court to return the ball. (The backcourt player must realize that the lobbed ball will bounce high, therefore necessitating a retreat well behind the baseline in order to let the ball drop down from the peak of its bounce to approximately waist level.) The ball is returned as a high lob, since the player realizes that both opponents are probably at the net and that his or her partner must have time to get back to the baseline.

Once both partners are side by side, either up at the net or back at the baseline, they stay side by side. If one goes back for an overhead, then the other also goes back. If one moves in for a short ball, the other moves in also.

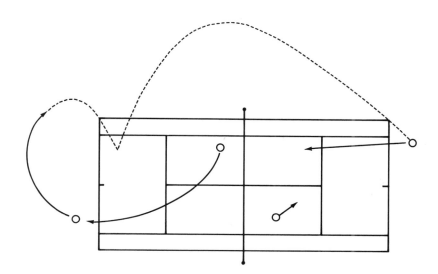

MORE ADVANCED DOUBLES STRATEGY

Doubles is an exciting and fast-moving game requiring great teamwork and communication between partners. You should keep this in mind when choosing a partner. You should also try to choose a partner whose style of play complements your own. (A quick-touch player and a more powerful partner often make a good team.)

Although the court in doubles play is 9 feet wider than in singles, two players can cover the entire area with comparative ease. Unlike singles, then, when you are hitting from the backcourt, the probability is low that you will be able to maneuver your opponents out of position; the angle to which to hit is just too limited. It is also unlikely that you will be able to use power as effectively from the backcourt, since from that position it is difficult to hit "through" two net players.

Strategy for the Serving Team

Who Should Serve First? Usually the best server should serve first in every set. Sometimes a special playing condition such as a tail wind or absence of sun glare will favor beginning with the weaker server. (Neither server should ever have to serve into the sun if one is left-handed and one is right-handed.)

Why the First Serve Is So Important. In doubles, fewer chances should be taken with the first serve than in singles, and more margin should be allowed (more spin, for example) to get the ball in play. A consistent first serve is important for three reasons: (1) The partner at the net can poach more effectively. (2) The server can come to the net more readily. An intermediate player should come to net on many first serves, but much less often on second serves. An advanced player will come to net on both serves, since the majority of points can be won by the team who gets to the net first. (3) The server has the strategic advantage. If the first serve is missed, however, the receiver will probably have an easier return on the second serve. (The second serve is usually hit with more safety and spin, which gives it a tendency to land short.) You can take fewer chances on the second serve, and the receiver knows it will probably be served to his or her backhand. Thus the receiver can gamble—run around his or her backhand, move in closer and quicker, hit harder, and so on. A short second serve lets the receiver join his or her partner at the net.

Considerations on When to Serve Wide. The most effective wide serves are the slice to the forehand in the deuce court and the twist to the backhand in the ad court. The wide serve can be effective when:

1. Your opponent is getting to the net off the return too quickly. A wide serve slows your opponent down by moving him or her wide for the return instead of forward.
2. Your opponent has trouble returning a wide shot.
3. Both opponents are behind the baseline. This tends to pull the receiver wide, opening up the court for the poach by the server's partner.

Considerations on When to Serve Down the Middle. The serve to the middle of the court in the *deuce court* is effective when served to the backhand. The ball served to the center of the court makes it easier for the server's partner to poach toward the center since it is more difficult for the opponent to return the ball to the alley. For this reason, in the deuce court the server's partner at the net will often begin the point standing closer to the center of the court, since the basic serve is to the backhand (middle of the court). In the ad court, the serve will probably be wider, so the partner often stands closer to the alley.
Serve down the middle to the *ad court* when:

1. Your opponent is "keying" for the usual serve to the backhand, especially on an "ad" point.
2. Your opponent overswings regularly on the forehand return. This ball can be served in tight to cramp the swing.
3. The receiver has a good angle return. This cuts down the return angle.

In either the deuce court or the ad court, a serve in tight to the body is good, especially on a second serve, since the receiver has little room to do much to the return.

The Poach. Poaching is a strategy in which the net player moves toward his or her partner's side of the court to intercept a return shot. The net player should always move diagonally forward on the poach to take the ball as close to the net as possible. The poaching net player aims the return shot at the opening between the receiver (who is back) and the net player, or slightly toward the net player's feet. If the poaching player's momentum carries him or her to the server's side of the court, the serving partner moves over to cover the poacher's original side.

If the serving team decides to poach often in a particular match, it may be advantageous for the net player to *signal* any intentions to his or her partner in advance. The net player can signal a stay, a poach, or a fake poach. The decision to poach now becomes an all-or-nothing commitment. If the poach signal has been given, the server must cover the partner's side immediately upon serving.

If you are the server on a team that poaches often, you might serve from a position closer to the center of the court. In order to protect against the angle return, serve more down the middle. The poach stands the best chance of being effective on the first serve, so concentrate on getting the first serve in and don't try a risky serve.

The poach is a good move when:

1. You are having trouble winning the point serving to a particular side of the court. In this case the poach can break the receiver's rhythm and keep the receiver from grooving the return. The receiver has many more things to think about against a poaching net player.

2. The point is a big one, such as "ad out." Here the poach can help the server out of a jam, especially if the server has had to struggle to win serve.

3. The serve is deep. If the ball lands near the service line, be ready to move.

4. The return is a floating underspin. This shot often lends itself to poaching, since the ball is rising.

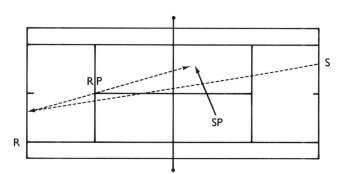

Play "Australian" Doubles. Another service strategy to counteract an effective return (specifically the wide-angle return on the backhand from the ad court) is for the server's partner to get positioned on the same side of the court as the server, where the cross-court return can be intercepted. The serve must be made from close to the center of the court so the server can move over to the opposite side to cover the territory usually covered by his or her partner.

If the serve is to the ad court, the net player starts at the net, on the left (instead of the right) side of the court. The serve is made from near the center on the left side, and the server moves to the right side to continue the point. This forces the receiver to return down the line, which is often difficult for the player with a good cross-court backhand. The maneuver may be tried on certain points to break the receiver's rhythm or to help get out of a particular jam.

The server's partner may opt to poach from the "center-of-the-court position." In this case, it is an especially good idea for the server to signal the partner of this intention before the serve.

If the server has an especially good volley on one side or is weak on the other, a team may use Australian doubles. For example, if Australian doubles is used when serving to the ad court, the server should never have to hit a backhand volley, since the server will be moving toward the forehand side of the court.

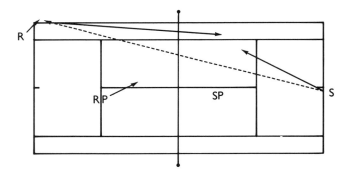

Try the Australian formation early in a match in which your team is comfortably ahead in a game (30-15, 40-0). Serve a consistent first serve to the backhand. (The server's partner should not poach the first time, since the serving team is just testing to see how well the receiver can return with a backhand down the line.) Remember how your opponent reacts. If the reaction is tentative and unsure, use the Australian formation any time you are in trouble (behind) in a game, until your opponent proves that he or she can return well down the line. If your opponent is aggressive on the return, however, you will use Australian more to change the receiver's rhythm than to get out of trouble.

Usually, Australian doubles is not used on a second serve, since the receiver will anticipate a serve to the backhand. If the receiver runs around it and hits a forehand, this return will be at the maximum angle and therefore stands a good chance to be an outright winner.

Strategy for the Receiving Team

Who Returns from Which Court? In determining which partner receives from the deuce court and which from the ad court, the prime consideration should be: Where does each receiver feel more comfortable? Usually a player with a natural underspin backhand will play the deuce (forehand) court, where most serves tend to be in close to the receiver's backhand. The partner with the better drive backhand (topspin) usually plays the ad (backhand) court, since there is more room on this side for a fuller return swing.

There are other factors to be considered as well. A left-handed player might play the ad court expecting that most serves will be directed to the backhands (or down the middle) and to keep both partners' forehands on the outside, where more reach is needed. Or the left-hander might play the deuce court to keep both forehands in the middle, where most balls are hit.

The stronger player might play the deuce court, where more points (at least half) are served (for example, the ad receiver returns one less point in a 40-15 game). Or the player who is better able to handle the pressure at "game" point may therefore play the ad court.

Hitting the Return. A good return of serve is one of the most important shots in doubles, for it sets the tempo of the point. In advanced doubles the receiver assumes that the server is coming to the net, so the receiver's goal is to keep the ball low to the approaching server in order to make the server volley up. On the return of serve, the receiver also will often come to the net, although the first rule is get the ball in play.

As receiver you should adjust your court position so you have the best chance to get the ball in play. For example, move back a little if you are having difficulty in returning a hard serve. The farther back you stand, the more you can swing and drive the return with topspin. (However, since you sacrifice being closer to the net, it will be just about impossible to get to net behind your return.) The closer in you stand, the more you must shorten your swing and block or chip the return (more underspin). This also gives you a better chance to protect against the poach, to hit down on the return, and to move in to the net to volley.

Against a poaching team, try a chip lob return to get the ball quickly over the poaching net player's head. If a team is known to poach often, start the match by hitting behind the poacher early so your opponents will know that you are not afraid to do so. If this still doesn't work, start the point with both partners on the baseline, for this gives the poacher less chance to be effective.

Against Australian doubles, the basic play is to take the ball early and hit aggressively down the line. If you have difficulty doing this, move your partner from the net to the backcourt with you, and perhaps even use lobs for your return. If the serving team plays Australian on their second serve, the ball will probably be served to your backhand, so run around it and crack a forehand return.

The Receiver's Partner. If you are the receiver's partner, you normally begin on the center of the service line. Your responsibility is to call the "out" serves and watch your partner's return. If the return is reasonably low and to the approaching server, move forward into a position about 10 feet from the net. If the return of serve is low and to the center of the court, you can poach to the center. (Be certain to move diagonally forward any time you poach.) If the return goes toward the net player (either because of a poor return or a poach) move back and toward the center to give yourself time to react and to cut off the opening in the middle of the court.

When Both Partners Are in the Backcourt

As the receiver's partner, you might choose to stand back at the baseline when:

1. The server's partner is poaching often (on first serves, for example) and effectively. The poacher is less able to hit an outright winner at your feet and between partners if you are back.

2. Your partner is having particular trouble with the return. With both partners back, the receiver has more margin—the low return is not so critical and the receiver can concentrate more on just getting the ball back.

3. The server is consistently beating the receiver to the net and by better positioning is winning the point on the first volley. (Play from the backcourt requires a less exacting return and makes it more difficult for the opposing server to put the first volley away for the winner.)

4. The serving team is a "groove" team and has established a fast pace and momentum. The receiving team should stay back and try to break the momentum. This can also be effective as a psychological maneuver on select points, such as the first two points of a game, if the serving team has been easily holding serve in the first part of the set.

5. You want to exploit an opponent's weak overhead or the weaker partner. In this situation, the receiver and partner stand substantially back and just try to get the ball in play on the return. Once it is in play, try to keep hitting to the

weaker player. If that player is at the net, start by alternating deep, high defensive lobs with aggressive topspin drives to make that player move up and back. (If the ball is returned short to you, then both you and your partner can take the offense by moving in to the net.)

Don't make the mistake of trying to overpower your opponents at the net. Be patient and try to keep the up-back (drive-lob) combination rally going until the volley or overhead is returned short enough for you to effectively hit hard in an attempt to win the point outright.

When Both Teams Are at the Net

The great majority (75 percent) of all points in advanced doubles end with all four players at the net, like in-fighting in boxing. While both teams are waiting for an offensive opportunity, the emphasis is on keeping the ball low. This often requires softer shots. Once one team hits the ball up, however, the opposing team moves in for the knockout punch, and volleys down.

Which Partner Is Responsible for Which Ball? In order to avoid opening up any unnecessary angles, most balls are hit down the middle when all four players are at the net. If you are moving in when a ball is returned down the middle, you should probably take the ball. If you have been pulled wide, your partner must move over and cover the middle. If your opponents are returning the wide ball, the partner on that side must cover the alley while the other partner covers the center. If neither player is moving, the player with the forehand in the middle will usually take the shot. If there is any doubt, go for the ball. Above all, don't be indecisive.

The Importance of Keeping the Ball Low. Return the low ball to the feet of the player farther from you. This cross-court volley gives the ball more time to drop to your opponent's feet. If you are successful in returning low, move in close, for your opponent must volley up and you will then be in a good position to volley down for the winner. Be aggressive and keep attacking. The farther back you stand, the easier it is for your opponents to hit to your feet. Try an extreme angle shot only if you can probably hit an outright winner. (Don't give your opponents an even greater angle for their return.)

What to Do When the Ball Is Returned High. If the ball is returned up to you, move in quickly and hit down at the feet of the opponent nearer to you. Anticipate the high ball by virtue of your low return. Start closing in even before your opponent hits the low return. The partner who is not hitting should be ready to back up the hitting player in case the opponents try a quick lob or lob volley. (The lob volley is a difficult shot, however, and will not often be successful.)

When Both Partners Are at the Net and the Opponents Are Back

Be Patient. Realize that the rallies will be longer and it will be harder to put the ball away. Don't try to power the ball past your opponents. Short, angled volleys can be effective, since they tend to pull one partner up and out of position. But, if you don't have enough angle to win the point outright, keep the ball deep and down the middle. This will keep your opponents back on defense, and confuse them a little about who will return the ball.

Expect the Lob. Play farther from the net. Fifteen feet from the net is not too far back for your home-base "set" position, especially if you are not too confident in your overhead. Try to hit every ball *before* it bounces. (Only an extremely high and short lob should be allowed to bounce.)

If a lob should get over your head, your partner should cross diagonally back from the net and try to return it with a high, defensive lob. You should also move to the backcourt, and cross over to your partner's original side of the court.

If you are hitting the overhead from deep in your court, hit with more spin and less power, and hit it more down the middle. Smash all short lobs and high balls hard and down the middle unless you have a tremendous angle. When both opponents are back you have a great chance to play the weaker player.

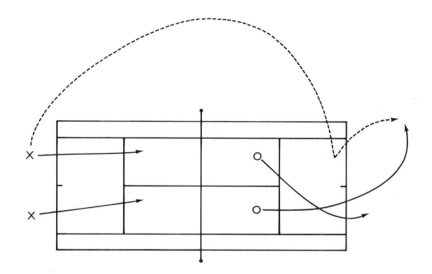

Practicing the Game: Drills for the More Advanced Player

DRILLS FOR THE SINGLES PLAYER

Success in sports is largely due to confidence. Confidence comes from knowing what you can and cannot do well in specific situations. Then you can play within your capabilities.

A systematic effort to turn your weaknesses into strengths will help you gain the confidence you need. Do a particular thing over and over again until its execution has become second nature. Start in simple, almost rote terms, like "groove" hitting with tossed balls or with a ball machine. Then progress into rallies with a partner, but with sequences that are still definable. Finally, "play the game," where you may have little control over the type and timing of situations that develop.

Most of all, realize that the game of tennis is difficult to learn to play well. It takes many meaningful hours, even years, of well-directed hard work to become a good tennis player. Be prepared to spend extra time on the court if you aspire high. (Fortunately, tennis practice can be not only challenging but fun.)

Backcourt Drills

Groove Hitting (Usually to a Target). With the help of a tossing partner or ball machine, practice *returning wide balls*. Start at the center of the court. Turn, by pushing off, and run to where the ball will be. Try to beat the ball to the spot. Emphasize adjusting your feet when you reach the hitting area. Return by side-skipping back to the center of the court. Practice forehands, then backhands. Then alternate forehands and backhands, or short balls and deep balls. Remember to take your racket back with your first step.

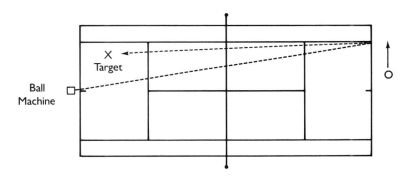

With the help of a hitting partner, do the following drills:

1. *Rally cross court* (forehand to forehand) *or down the line* (forehand to backhand). Begin in the service court and move back to full court as your control improves. Emphasize depth when at full court, so that all balls land beyond the service line. Try to return to the center mark after each shot.

2. *Rally cross court and down the line* (player A hits only cross-court shots; player B hits only down-the-line shots). Begin in the service court and then move gradually back to the backcourt. Hit three-quarter speed, and try not to hit too close to the line. The emphasis is on keeping the rally going as long as possible. When you are hurried, put more arc on your return. Try to keep the ball deep (beyond the service line).

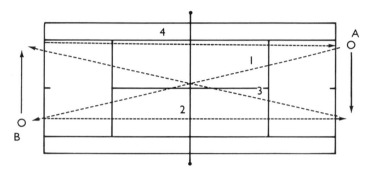

Game-type Playing Drills. The following drills have no pattern.

1. Playing points:

   a. A beginner may start by using the service squares. A better player would use the full court. Play until one player wins 10 points. Concentrate on being steady.

   b. As a variation of the above, play until one player makes "two more errors than placements." Play rally points, with each of your errors counting as "minus 1" and each of your placements counting as "plus 1." You lose the game if you commit two more errors than placements before your opponent does. If one player gets pulled to the net, he or she should hit defensive volleys only. Emphasize changing pace, changing direction, and changing spin.

2. Emphasizing the approach shot:

   a. Begin with a backcourt rally and come in on the first short ball. Either play "points" or play "two more errors than placements."

   b. Begin with a cross-court rally. Both players start in the backcourt. When a short ball is hit to you, move in and hit an approach shot down the line. The backcourt player tries to pass the net rusher.

3. Emphasizing the passing shot:

   a. *Three-on-one passing shots.* Player A hits ball (1) to player D's backhand and comes to net. Player D hits the passing shot (2). Player A then volleys the ball to the other side of the court (3). Player B repeats player A's pattern. After several cycles, players A, B, and C direct the first ball to player D's forehand. Finally, players A, B, and C alternate hitting the first ball to player D's forehand and backhand.

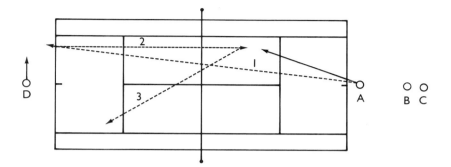

b. *Instructor feeds.* An "instructor" stands at the net post, just off the court, and feeds a short ball to the backcourt player. The player hits an approach shot and comes to net. The opponent tries to pass the net rusher. Repeat the process.

c. *Four-hit passing shot.* Player A is at the net on one side of the court with a bucket of balls. The player begins a four-hit cycle by putting the ball in play down the line (1). Player B returns the ball to the net player (2), who then volleys the ball cross court (3). Player B then runs over and hits the passing shot down the line (4). The cycle begins again as player A quickly puts another ball in play down the line.

The cycle can be repeated by having player A hit the first ball cross court, in which case player B will end up hitting a cross-court passing shot on the fourth ball.

Player A then can move to the other side of the court to repeat both cycles. Remember, the second ball is always returned to the net player.

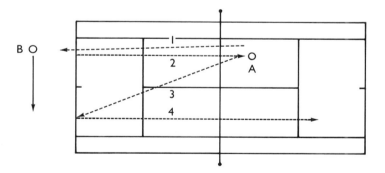

Net Play Drills

Groove Hitting. With the help of a tossing partner or a ball machine, practice returning the following:

1. *Volleys.* Start with forehands, switch to backhands, and finally, get into wider volleys.

2. *Overheads.*

3. *Alternated wide volleys*—a forehand, followed by a backhand.

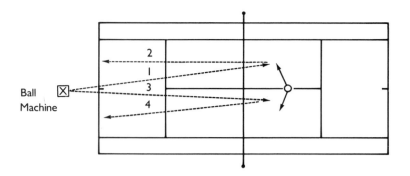

4. *A 3-hit cycle.* Player A feeds three shots—(1) a short ball, (2) a wide volley, and (3) a wide volley—to the other side. Player B, beginning at the baseline, hits a forehand approach shot and moves toward the net. Player B then hits a backhand first volley and moves closer to the net to put away a forehand volley. Player B then returns to the back of the line. Player C repeats the 3-hit cycle, but begins with a backhand approach shot, follows with a forehand first volley, and ends with a backhand volley. This drill may also be done using a ball machine.

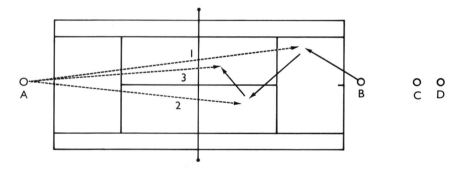

1. *Volley wide balls.* One player is at the backcourt and the other at the net. Use only one side of the court and return to the center mark each time. The volleyer hits forehand volleys only, and only to the backcourt player's backhand, or vice versa.

2. *Alternate volleys* (cross court, down the line). The backcourt player hits only down the line, and the volleyer hits only cross court. Keep the ball in play rather than trying to win the point.

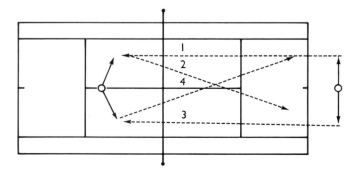

3. *Volley rally.* Both players are at the net and volley either straight ahead to each other or, standing slightly off-center, diagonally across the court.

4. *Practice net approach.* Both players start just in front of the baseline. With each shot, both move forward a bit. By the third or fourth shot, both players are at the net in a continuous volley rally.

5. *Volley single file.* One player is at the net and keeps one ball in play, while four or five other players are in a single-file line on the opposite side of the net. The players follow each other up to the net to hit a volley and then go back to the end of the line. If a shot is missed, another ball is quickly fed to keep the approach rhythm going.

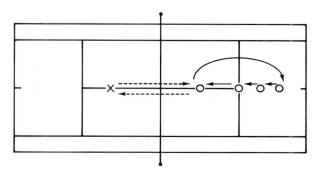

6. *Practice overheads* (player A is in the backcourt; player B is at the net).

   a. Player A lobs. Player B hits overheads.

   b. "Up and back": Player A alternates (1) drives with (3) deep, high lobs, keeping all balls down the center of the court. Player B (2) moves in for the volley and then (4) moves quickly back for the overhead. Try to keep the ball in play.

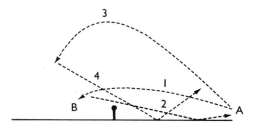

Game-type Playing Drills. The following drills have no pattern.

1. *One side of the court only.* One player is positioned at the net, the other player is back. Both players try to win the point, one by using a combination of lobs and passing shots, the other by using the volley and overhead.

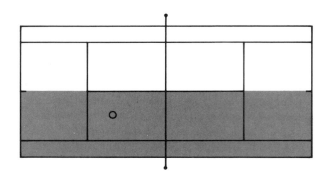

2. *Australian two-on-one.*

   a. Two players on the same side of the net start at the net. The third player is in the backcourt on the opposite side of the net. The net players try to hit so the backcourt player can barely get to the shots. The backcourt player should not overhit but should try to make each shot simulate a passing shot, keeping the balls out of the middle and trying to take the short balls as early and aggressively as possible.

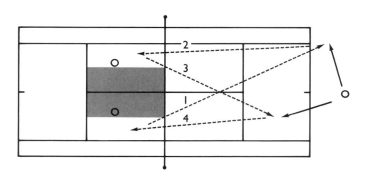

   b. Two players start in the backcourt on one side of the net, with the third player on the opposite side of the net, at the net. The backcourt players try to move the net player around as much as possible, using a lot of lobs. The net player should be able to just reach almost every ball.

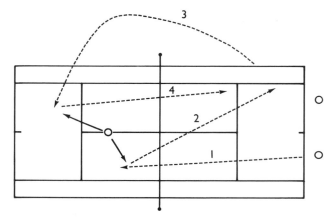

3. *The "scramble."* Player A serves and comes to net. Player B, who has a bucket of balls, disregards the balls player A hits and instead uses balls from the bucket to feed net player A one shot after another for approximately a 12-shot sequence. The object is to make player A hit the first volley and then move quickly from side to side and up and back for hard drives, lobs, and soft balls. A variation is for player B to start by moving player A from side to side in the backcourt and then to feed a short ball so that player A can work on an approach to the net off the ground rather than off the serve.

Serve and Serve Return Drills

Always keep in mind the great importance of practicing all types of serves. Also remember that whenever one person is practicing a serve, someone else can be practicing a return. Practice serving different types of serves to different parts of the court.

1. *Two-on-one serve and volley* (players A and C serve; player B returns). Use second serves only and work on one type of return at a time (such as chip, drive, standing in close, standing back).

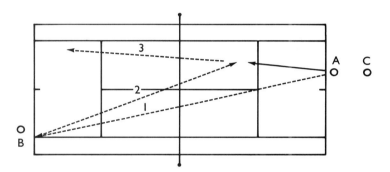

2. *Four-hit serve and volley.* (1) Player A serves to the deuce court. (2) Player B returns the ball so that (3) player A (server) can volley to the ad court. (4) Player B then goes for the passing shot. The sequence is repeated, except player A serves the next ball to the ad court. Player B then returns from the ad court and passes from the deuce court.

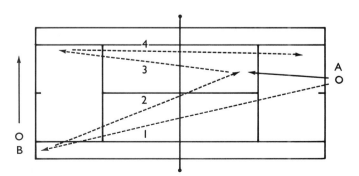

3. *Play points to 10* or until one player makes two more errors than placements, using the serve and volley.

4. *Serve for four games* or until you are broken (the receiver uses one theme for the entire four-game series—chip or soft returns, drive returns and lob, moving in on second serves or running around them, and so on); or serve until you make two errors.

DRILLS FOR DOUBLES

Basic Situations

The Cross-Court Rally: The Net Players Move with the Ball. Both teams take basic positions, with one partner at net and the other partner in the backcourt. Backcourt players begin a cross-court rally.

1. Backcourt players (A and D) keep the ball away from the net players, and hit the ball high enough over the net to keep it deep. (You will soon see how the high, bouncing deep ball either sets up the poach for your partner or elicits a short return on which you can move into the net.)

2. Net players (B and C) slide with each shot to the side of court the ball is on, always watching the ball. Remember to first cover your respective alley but also to look for the poach.

3. The net players try to intercept ("poach") any ball they can, in which case the opposing net player covers toward the center of the court.

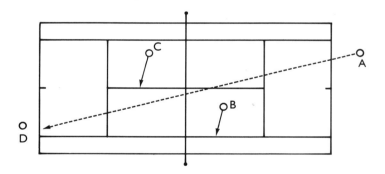

The Cross-Court Rally: The Short Ball. If the ball lands short, the backcourt player (A) moves up to it and continues to the net to join partner. Both partners (A and B) assume the new home-base position just inside the service line.

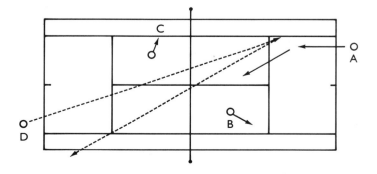

The Lob: The Short Lob. Start the point with the basic cross-court rally. After two or three returns, player A tries lobbing over the opposing net player. If the lob is short, the lobber's partner (B) retreats toward the baseline but gets set as player C smashes the ball, and the smasher's partner (D) joins player C at the net at the new home base.

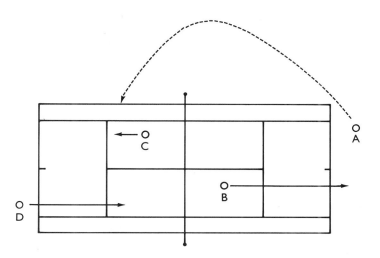

The Lob: The Deep Lob. If the lob is deep and clears the net player's head:

1. The net player (C) yells "switch" and crosses diagonally to the other side of the court toward the baseline.

2. The net player's partner (D) covers, by crossing behind the baseline in an attempt to return the ball with a high, deep lob.

3. The original player hitting the lob (A) joins partner B in the new home base at the net.

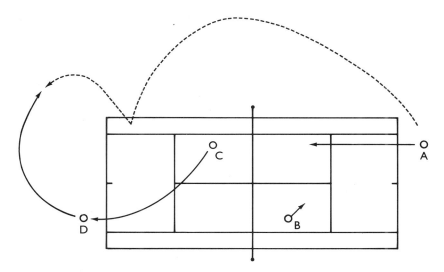

Using the Serve and Serve Return. Use the serve and serve return and continue to play points. Analyze where you are standing after each point to be certain you are in the proper position on the court for whatever situation has occurred. The receiver's partner (C) should be positioned at the service line when the ball is served but should be ready to move up to the proper home base at the net if the return goes back to the server.

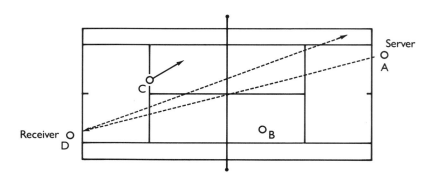

More Advanced Drills for Doubles

With an Instructor.

1. *Poaching.* Three players stand in single file on one side of the net and toward the back of the court. Player A runs in toward the net. As Player A begins to split stop, the instructor hits a ball cross court. Player A moves diagonally forward to volley it, then returns to the back of the line as Player B repeats the procedure.

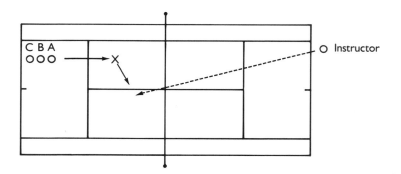

2. *Doubles "drop out" I.* One team (A) is at the net and the other team (B) is at the baseline. Teams C and D wait behind Team B. The instructor, standing just off the court at the net post, feeds a ball to Team B, and the point begins. (Team B will use many lobs, since their opponents are at the net.) If Team B wins the point, they replace Team A at the net and play the next point against Team C. If Team A wins the point, however, Team B drops out and Team C replaces them.

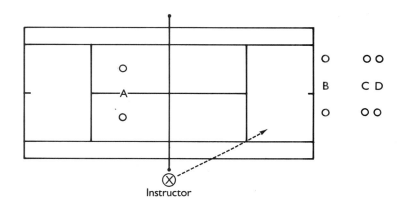

Instructor

3. *Doubles "drop out" II.* As above, but Team A and Team B both start at the net.

4. *Six-player volley rally.* Three players are on one side of the net, and two additional players flank the instructor on the other side. The instructor in the middle has a bucket of balls and starts the rally by hitting the ball anywhere on the other side. The rally is played to completion.

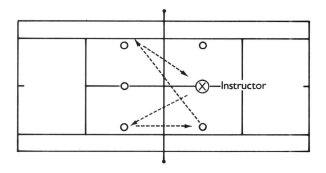

With Only One Other Player.

1. *Two-player doubles—the attack.* (Players use only diagonally opposite sides of the court.) The server hits a second serve (one serve only) and comes to the net. The receiver returns and also comes in. Play full speed, and play the point to completion. Use soft, low volleys to get your opponent to volley up to you so you can move in and put the ball away.

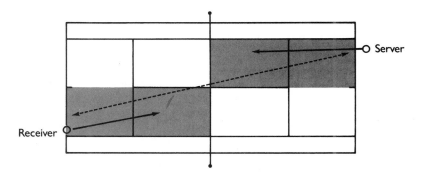

2. *Two-player doubles—the defense.* The server both serves and volleys cross court. The receiver defends by staying back after the return, and "works" the point by mixing high, deep lobs and drives. (All balls must go diagonally cross court.)

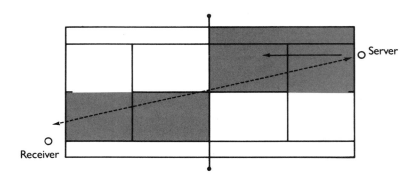

Practice Game-like Situations. It is important not only to practice drills, but also to practice in more game-like situations, especially ones you will have to adapt to in certain conditions and in certain matches. Practice the following situations as both the serving team and the receiving team: (1) Australian doubles and (2) with both members of the receiving team staying in the backcourt.

PHYSICAL CONDITIONING FOR THE TENNIS PLAYER

A physical conditioning program should accomplish two goals: It should increase your ability to perform maximally over time, and it should greatly minimize the chance of injury. The body that is in shape can handle maximum physical exertion with minimal effort. The increase in physical efficiency both delays fatigue and hastens recovery from fatigue. Any fatigue—momentary or lingering—not only hinders maximum performance, but makes you more susceptible to injury.

Most tennis injuries are either pulled muscles or injured joints. Tennis is an extremely strenuous game. Often we demand more of our body than it is prepared to endure. We tend to get careless about staying in condition and lazy about proper warmup. A good warmup is especially important on cold days, on the day after a strenuous match (when some residual stiffness is likely), and for those who have not played tennis in a number of years.

The frequency of muscle pulls can be minimized with 3 or 4 minutes of light jogging to raise internal body temperature. This should be followed by stretching just before play begins. Some people are naturally more susceptible to pulling a muscle than others. But everyone should take time to slowly stretch out the muscle groups that commonly cause problems. After your match is over, stay warm, especially if you have another match to play. If you feel a muscle starting to get tight or to pull, immediately cover it with an icebag to decrease swelling from any internal bleeding that might have occurred. Remember that recovery from a muscle pull can be slow, so don't be impatient to return to unlimited activity.

The usual knee and ankle injuries are sprains resulting from twisting. If you have weak ankles, it may be necessary to wear high-top shoes or even to tape the ankle before play to give it extra support. For weak knees, an elastic wrapping may serve as sufficient added support.

Of the joints in the upper body, the shoulders are a common problem. If you are insufficiently warmed up, certain shots—especially overheads and serves—can tear fibers in the shoulder and cause internal hemorrhaging. Such an injury can lead to severe problems later on, including calcium deposits, which could require surgical removal. Take extra care to hit many easy practice serves and overheads. Take swings, even without a ball, to simulate above-the-shoulder motions and to properly warm up this joint. You would not start your car cold and immediately drive it at 80 miles per hour; you'd let the engine idle a few minutes to warm it up and to get the oil circulating. Treat your shoulder the same way.

The elbow joint is a particular curse among tennis players. "Tennis elbow" has become increasingly common as more and more people in middle age take up the game. This *tendonitis*, or inflammation of the tendon, can be largely eliminated with gradual and proper warmup for all kinds of shots. Hitting the ball incorrectly can cause tennis elbow. Players especially susceptible are those who hyperextend the elbow on their backhand or who use excessive wrist roll and jerkiness on their forehand. Proper hitting can partly be defined as "letting the racket do the work for you." In other words, if the swing is efficient, the momentum of the racket head will impart speed to the ball, rather than the player having to "body" or force the shot.

Exercise great care at even the slightest sign of strain in the elbow or shoulder. If the pain or heaviness persists, you might try a racket with a lighter head and looser strings. Or you might use softer balls, to minimize the shock as racket meets ball. You might even try "choking up" on the racket handle a little. After play, immediately apply an icepack to the inflamed area.

Stomach muscle pulls and back injuries are also quite common. A serve ball tossed too far back over the head (such as with the American twist serve) is usually the cause. To help prevent such injuries, use curl-ups to strengthen the stomach (abdominal) muscles and to give stronger support to your back.

Don't try to be a hero or heroine. If an injury persists, see your doctor for professional diagnosis and advice. Take good care of your body, as you would any piece of valuable machinery, and you will be able to enjoy this beautiful game for a lifetime.

The physical conditioning program depicted on the following pages emphasizes:

1. Warmup, jogging, and stretching—for increased flexibility
2. Interval training—for increased cardiovascular efficiency
3. Weight training—for muscular strength and endurance

A Stretching and Warmup Program

A sample stretching exercise is presented for each of the main muscle groups of the body. This should help increase your body's flexibility and thus make it less susceptible to muscle pulls. Remember to stretch slowly and smoothly throughout the full range of each movement.

1. Shoulders (Deltoid muscles) (Arms over head)

2. Shoulders (Deltoid muscles) (Arms behind back)

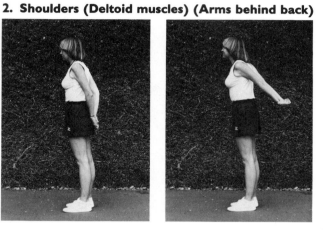

3. Trunk (Abdominals and latissimus dorsi)

4. Thigh (Quadraceps)

5. Calf (Gastrocnemius)

6. Groin

7. Hamstrings

You might try a couple of simple exercises while on the court to help strengthen key parts of your body: curl-ups for the abdominals and push-ups for the upper arm.

Curl-Ups

Push-Ups

Your cardiovascular efficiency and general body warmup can be enhanced by jumping rope and by jogging. "Follow-the-leader" agility drills on the court take only a limited amount of time and, when combined with short sprints across several courts, can help your overall conditioning.

Jump Rope

"Up" Agility Drill

"Back" Agility Drill

"Side" Agility Drill

A Weight-Training Program

More and more athletes have access to weight-training equipment, either through school or at health and fitness centers. Weight training can increase speed, explosive power, flexibility, and muscular endurance. A good general workout for a tennis player can be accomplished in 30 minutes. There should be at least 48 hours, but no more than 96 hours, between workouts. (Once a certain strength level is reached, 95 percent of it can be retained with one workout a week.)

Weight training consists of a series of resistance exercises for specific muscle groups of the body. A particular exercise should be repeated at least 8, and up to 12, times. Each repetition is referred to as a rep. If you cannot do 8 reps, the weight is too heavy. If you can do more than 12 reps, the weight is too light.

The rate for performing each rep should be about 2 seconds up, about 4 seconds down. Use a full range of motion. If a rep takes 5–6 seconds to complete, the entire exercise set will last about a minute. No more than a minute of rest should be taken before moving on to the next exercise. You should keep a record of the weight used and the number of reps achieved for each exercise. This helps you to monitor your improvement.

The following exercises are selected especially for tennis players. There are several kinds of weight equipment available. For the sake of simplicity, most of the following exercises are performed on the Nautilus machines. The type of machine, order of exercise, and muscle groups affected are listed.

Machine	Order of Exercise	Muscle Groups
a. Hydra Gym	1. Abduction/Adduction	Groin
b. Nautilus Leg Extension	2. Leg extension	Quadraceps
c. Nautilus Leg Curl	3. Leg curl	Hamstrings
d. Nautilus Double Shoulder	4. Side lateral raise	Deltoids
	5. Seated press	Deltoids (triceps)
e. Nautilus Double Chest	6. Bent arm fly	Pectorals
	7. Decline press	Pectorals (deltoids, triceps)
f. Nautilus Pullover	8. Pullover	Latissimus dorsi
	9. Lateral pulldown	Latissimus dorsi (biceps)
g. Nautilus Bicep-Tricep	10. Biceps curl	Biceps
	11. Triceps extension	Triceps
h. Universal Curl	12. Wrist curls	Wrist flexors (forearms)
	13. Wrist reverse curls	Wrist extensors (forearms)

An Interval-Training Program

Tennis is primarily an anaerobic activity. That is, since tennis demands relatively short, explosive bursts of energy (as opposed to the more sustained energy use of distance swimming and jogging), the tennis player's body must be trained to withstand fatigue for short activity periods with decreased oxygen supply.

The most efficient method by which to achieve this condition is *interval training,* which consists of high-intensity running over prescribed distances with prescribed rest periods. Most running is done for distances of 220 yards and 440 yards, with supplemental runs of 110 yards and 660 yards.

The 110- and 220-yard runs require a period of relief (in other words, active rest, like a fast walk or easy jog) about three times the duration of the run. The 440- and 660-yard runs require a relief time of about twice the duration of the run. (Complete inactivity between running bouts will result only in early fatigue.)

Interval training can take place every other day (a day's rest is needed for the body to recover) or twice a week, but the total distance run is increased each week. Here follows a sample eight-week schedule that builds from one mile to a total distance of two miles. You should time yourself with a stopwatch each day. (If you are not in reasonable condition when you begin interval training, you may wish to start with a reduced schedule totaling from one-half to three-quarters of a mile.) Remember to always have a "cool-down" period at the end—some light jogging or walking. (Once a certain strength level is reached, 95 percent of it can be retained with one workout a week.)

Week 1 (1 mile; 1760 yards)
Tuesday: 2 × 440; 2 × 220; 4 × 110
Thursday: 1 × 660; 1 × 440; 3 × 220

Week 2 ($1\frac{1}{8}$ mile; 1980 yards)
Tuesday: 2 × 440; 3 × 220; 4 × 110
Thursday: 2 × 660; 3 × 220

Week 3 ($1\frac{1}{4}$ mile; 2200 yards)
Tuesday: 2 × 440; 4 × 220; 4 × 110
Thursday: 2 × 660; 4 × 220

Week 4 ($1\frac{3}{8}$ mile; 2420 yards)
Tuesday: 2 × 440; 4 × 220; 6 × 110
Thursday: 2 × 660; 1 × 440; 3 × 220

Week 5 ($1\frac{1}{2}$ mile; 2640 yards)
Tuesday: 2 × 440; 4 × 220; 8 × 110
Thursday: 2 × 660; 2 × 440; 2 × 220

Week 6 ($1\frac{5}{8}$ mile; 2860 yards)
Tuesday: 3 × 440; 3 × 220; 8 × 110
Thursday: 2 × 660; 2 × 440; 3 × 220

Week 7 ($1\frac{3}{4}$ mile; 3080 yards)
Tuesday: 3 × 440; 4 × 220; 8 × 110
Thursday: 2 × 660; 2 × 440; 4 × 220

Week 8 (2 miles; 3520 yards)
Tuesday: 4 × 440; 4 × 220; 8 × 110
Thursday: 2 × 660; 3 × 440; 4 × 220

Organizing Your Practice Workout

Approximately three hours a day, five days a week, affords enough time for any individual to improve to his or her highest level, provided the time is used wisely. Although the total time may vary from individual to individual and the time allotment may vary according to the nearness of competition dates, you cannot go far wrong by spending approximately half of every day's workout engaged in practice drills (mixing groove hitting with playing-type drills) and the other half in playing (points, games, or sets; alternating singles and doubles). Select those drills (from the previous text section) that provide isolated work on backcourt play (groundstrokes), net play, serving, and receiving. A brief warmup period should include some jogging or jumping rope as well as stretching exercises. At the conclusion of practice, a 15-minute conditioning period might include curl-ups, push-ups, short sprints, and agility drills, or a 30-minute conditioning period might include weight training and interval training on alternate days. A sample five-day workout schedule follows.

Time	Drill	Monday	Tuesday	Wednesday	Thursday	Friday
2:00	Warmup (Jog; stretch)	Warmup (Jog; stretch)	Warmup (Jog; stretch)	Warmup (Jog; stretch)	Warmup (Jog; stretch)	Warmup (Jog; stretch)
2:15	Serve; return	Serve; return	Serve; return	Serve; return	Serve; return	Serve; return
2:30	Groundstrokes	1. Alternate forehands and backhands 2. Passing shot drill (4-hit: serve and volley; return and pass)	Australian two on one (passing shots)	1. Cross court/ down the line 2. Cross court rally (attack on short ball)	Backcourt points (attack on short ball)	1. Alternate forehands and backhands 2. Passing shot drill (partner at net feeds balls)
3:15	Net Play	1. Cross court/ down the line (one up; one back) 2. Scramble	1. Up-back (4-hit cycle) 2. Doubles points (both close)	1. Alternate forehand and backhand volleys 2. Scramble	1. Net approach (both partners start at baseline) 2. Volley rally 3. Doubles points (one player back)	1. Approach net and volley (3-hit cycle) 2. Scramble
4:00	Play	Singles (sets)	Doubles	Singles (points/games)	Doubles	Singles (sets)
4:45	Conditioning	Weights	Intervals	Weights	Intervals	Weights

Organization of Tennis

ADMINISTRATIVE ORGANIZATION

The United States Tennis Association (U.S.T.A.)
51 E. 42nd Street
New York, NY 10017
(212) 949-9112

The United States is divided into 17 geographic sections, all governed by the United States Tennis Association, but each responsible for promoting and governing tennis in its own area. Groupings in local and national competition are by sex and age: youths—under 12, 14, 16, 18, and 21; men—over 35, 50, 55, 60, 65, 70, 75, and 80; women—over 35, 40, 45, 50, 55, 60, 65, and 70. Events include singles and doubles and sometimes mixed doubles.

Youths may enter a specific age group only if they have not reached the maximum age in that group by October 1 of the year of competition. An adult may play in an age group if he or she reaches the minimum age any time in the year of competition.

Each section has almost weekly competition in most events during the playing season—which means almost the entire year in some climates. Regular "circuits" of play are established within and between sections, and local and national rankings in each category are published yearly. Information regarding competition opportunities can be obtained from each section's headquarters. All active tennis players should be members of the U.S.T.A. For membership information, contact the New York office or one of the sectional associations.

U.S.T.A. SECTIONAL ADDRESSES

Caribbean Tennis Association
P.O. Box 40456, Minillas Station
Santurce, PR 00940
(809) 721-9112 or (809) 722-1655

Eastern Tennis Association
202 Mamaroneck Avenue
White Plains, NY 10601
(914) 946-3533

Florida Tennis Association
9620 Northeast 2nd Avenue, Room 209
Miami Shores, FL 33138
(305) 757-8568

Hawaii Tennis Association
P.O. Box 411
Honolulu, HI 96809
(808) 395-2291

Intermountain Tennis Association
2903 Laredo Place
Billings, MT 59102
(406) 656-9555

Mid-Atlantic Tennis Association
P.O. Drawer F
Springfield, VA 22151
(703) 321-9045

Middle States Tennis Association
939 Radnor Road
Wayne, PA 19087
(215) 688-4040

Missouri Valley Tennis Association
3724 16th Street
Des Moines, IA 50313
(515) 282-6712

New England Lawn Tennis Association
P.O. Box 223
Needham, MA 02192
(617) 444-1332

Northern California Tennis Association
645 5th Street
San Francisco, CA 94107
(415) 777-5683

Northwestern Tennis Association
2200 First Bank Place E.
Minneapolis, MN 55402
(612) 340-2913

Pacific Northwest Tennis Association
01875 S.W. Palatine Road
Portland, OR 97219
(503) 636-7847

Southern California Tennis Association
c/o Los Angeles Tennis Center
P.O. Box 240015
Los Angeles, CA 90024
(213) 208-3838

Southern Tennis Association
3121 Maple Drive N.E., Room 29
Atlanta, GA 30305
(404) 237-1319

Southwestern Tennis Association
3739 South Siesta
Tempe, AZ 85282
(602) 838-6788

Texas Tennis Association
P.O. Box 192
Austin, TX 78767
(512) 443-1334

Western Tennis Association
2215 Olympic Street
Springfield, OH 45503
(513) 390-2740

OTHER MAJOR ORGANIZATIONS

U.S.T.A. Education and Research Committee
729 Alexander Road
Princeton, NJ 08540
(609) 452-2580

This organization serves as the official resource center of the U.S.T.A. It is dedicated to help everyone interested in tennis—coaches, teachers, administrators—anyone promoting tennis as a lifetime sport. It provides lists of publications and films as well as information on facilities and is active in sponsoring teacher training workshops and grass-root programs in parks and schools.

U.S. Professional Tennis Association, Inc. (U.S.P.T.A.)
c/o Saddlebrook
P.O. Box 7077
Wesley Chapel (Tampa), FL 34249
(813) 973-3777

This organization of certified U.S. teaching professionals promotes the profession of teaching tennis and administers an extensive professional teacher "certification" program.

The Association of Tennis Professionals (A.T.P.)
319 Country Club Road
Garland, TX 75040
(214) 494-5991

This organization of the top male tennis playing professionals is instrumental in the administration of the men's professional tournament circuit and concerns itself with the conduct and welfare of its members.

Women's Tennis Association (W.T.A.)
1604 Union Street
San Francisco, CA 94123
(415) 441-1041

This organization of female tennis playing professionals is responsible for the women's professional circuit and promotes the tennis welfare of its members.

Intercollegiate Tennis Coaches Association (I.T.C.A.)
P.O. Box 71
Princeton, NJ 08544
(609) 452-6332

This organization of men's and women's college and community college coaches promotes the collegiate game and the coaches' profession.

The International Tennis Federation (I.T.F.)
Church Road, Wimbledon
London SW19 5TF
England

This is the governing body of international tennis, and it establishes the rules of tennis. The U.S.T.A. is a member of this organization.

TENNIS PUBLICATIONS

International Tennis Weekly
319 Country Club Road
Garland, TX 75040

This is the official weekly newspaper of the Association of Tennis Professionals. It includes professional tournament schedules, results, and latest computerized rankings of male professionals.

Inside Women's Tennis
1604 Union Street
San Francisco, CA 94123

This is the official weekly publication of the Women's Tennis Association. It includes professional tournament schedules, results, and latest computerized rankings for women.

Tennis Magazine
495 Westport Ave.
Norwalk, CT 06856

Although Tennis Magazine is officially endorsed by the U.S.P.T.A., it is a magazine for the general tennis fan. It is published monthly by Golf Digest/Tennis, Inc.

Tennis, USA Magazine
1515 Broadway
New York, NY 10036

This official publication of the U.S.T.A. contains human-interest stories, reports of age-group competition as well as of major tennis events, and sectional news, rankings, and results. Published monthly by CBS Publications and sent to all members of the U.S.T.A.

U.S.T.A. Yearbook
156 Broad Street
Lynn, MA 01901

The yearbook contains complete tennis rules, U.S.T.A. age-group rankings, championship results, sectional information and member club address lists, and historical results of the world's top events. Published by H. O. Zimman, Inc.

World Tennis Magazine
1515 Broadway
New York, NY 10036

This magazine is endorsed as the official publication of the U.S.T.A., and like *Tennis Magazine*, is a general-interest magazine for the tennis fan. Published monthly by CBS Publications.

COMPETITIONS

Until recently, tournaments of any consequence were open only to amateurs (players ineligible to receive prize money). The limited number of professionals (usually the best one or two amateurs each year "turned pro" in order to play for money) played mostly barnstorming exhibition matches throughout the world. Tournaments, in order to secure the best players, paid so much "under the table" to attract the top amateurs that many amateurs were actually making more money than the pros. In an effort to end this hypocrisy, the British, in 1968, opened Wimbledon—the most important tournament in the world and first held in 1877—to amateurs and professionals alike, and also offered prize money. Since then, all major international tournaments have been opened to professionals as well as amateurs (mostly college students and younger, who are ineligible for prize money). Another major development has been an increase in the number of major tournaments being played indoors, which has truly made tennis a year-round sport for spectators as well as players.

Major World Team Competitions

Davis Cup (established in 1900). Every country annually sends their top male players to this competition. The top 16 teams participate in a single elimination tournament—the World Group—for the championship, while the remaining countries play in four zonal groupings. Each of the zonal winners is promoted to the World Group for the following year's competition. The eight teams that lose in the first round of the World Group have a play-off in the order of the original draw. The four losers of this play-off are relegated to competition in their respective zones for the following year's competition, while the four winners remain in the World Group. Play consists of four singles matches and one doubles match.

Wightman Cup (established in 1923). This trophy is awarded annually to the winner of a dual match between British and American women. Play consists of five singles and two doubles matches.

Federation Cup (established in 1963). The International Lawn Tennis Federation initiated this international team competition for women. One nation plays another (two singles, one doubles) in a single elimination tournament at one site during one week.

The Olympics. Tennis was included in the Olympics from 1896 until 1924. It will reappear as a full official sport in the 1988 Olympic Games.

Age-Group Competitions. There are several established international age-group team competitions for juniors and adults.

Major Individual Competitions

The top international tournaments (now all "open" events) are the All-England Championships (Wimbledon), the United States Championships (Flushing Meadows, New York), the French Championships, and the Australian Championships (this last is of decreasing importance). Play consists of single elimination-type competition. Only five players have ever completed a "grand slam" by winning all four tournaments in succession: Don Budge, Maureen Connolly, and Martina Navratilova of the United States, and Rod Laver (twice) and Margaret Smith Court of Australia.

Professionally, both men and women now compete in year-round Grand Prix "circuits" during which they accumulate points that can lead to bonus prize money at the end of the year. Play is indoors and out, and on all types of surfaces. There are several tiers of competition. Satellite circuits and qualifying tournaments give lesser players a chance to work their way up to the major events. Computer points based on weekly results are awarded, and form the basis for rankings, which, for the most part, determine tournament eligibility.

There are circuits and tournaments for every age group in the United States. The "older" junior events, in addition to sectional play, feature a "national circuit" in the summer months. All outdoor national junior championships include a "feed-in" consolation event up through the quarter-finals.

Other Competitions

Beginning tennis players are often faced with the problem of finding practice partners and opponents of comparable ability. Many city recreation departments oversee public tennis clubs for adults that offer various levels of competition for a nominal annual fee. Many areas have tennis patron organizations that promote all levels of competition for youths.

The National Tennis Rating System

The U.S.T.A. has developed a self-rating system to help individuals determine their relative level of play for school, club, and community programs as well as for leagues and tournaments. The *National Tennis Rating Program* categories follow. (To "rate" yourself, assume you are playing someone of the same sex and ability.)

1.0 This player is just starting to play tennis.

1.5 This player has limited playing experience and is still working primarily on getting the ball over the net; has some knowledge of scoring but is not familiar with basic positions and procedures for singles and doubles play.

2.0 This player may have had some lessons but needs on-court experience; has obvious stroke weaknesses but is beginning to feel comfortable with singles and doubles play.

2.5 This player has more dependable strokes and is learning to judge where the ball is going; has weak court coverage or is often caught out of position, but is starting to keep the ball in play with other players of the same ability.

3.0 This player can place shots with moderate success; can sustain a rally of slow pace but is not comfortable with all strokes; lacks control when trying for power.

3.5 This player has achieved stroke dependability and direction on shots within reach, including forehand and backhand volleys, but still lacks depth and variety; seldom double faults and occasionally forces errors on the serve.

4.0 This player has dependable strokes on both forehand and backhand sides; has the ability to use a variety of shots including lobs, overheads, approach shots, and volleys; can place the first serve and force some errors; is seldom out of position in a doubles game.

4.5 This player has begun to master the use of power and spins; has sound footwork; can control depth of shots and is able to move opponent up and back; can hit first serves with power and accuracy and place the second serve; is able to rush net with some success on serve in singles as well as doubles.

5.0 This player has good shot anticipation; frequently has an outstanding shot or exceptional consistency around which a game may be structured; can regularly hit winners or force errors off of short balls; can successfully execute lobs, drop shots, half volleys, and overhead smashes; has good depth and spin on most second serves.

5.5 This player can execute all strokes offensively and defensively; can hit dependable shots under pressure; is able to analyze opponents' styles and can employ patterns of play to assure the greatest possibility of winning points; can hit winners or force errors with both first and second serves. Return of serve can be an offensive weapon.

6.0 This player has mastered all of the above skills; has developed power and/or consistency as a major weapon; can vary strategies and styles of play in a competitive situation. This player typically has had intensive training for national competition at junior or collegiate levels.

6.5 This player has mastered all of the above skills and is an experienced tournament competitor who regularly travels for competition and whose income may be partially derived from prize winnings.

7.0 This is a world class player.

Glossary

Ace. A ball that is served so well that the opponent has no chance to touch or return it.

Ad. Short for "advantage." It is the first point scored after deuce. If the serving side scores, it is "ad in"; if the receiving side scores, it is "ad out."

Ad court. The left-hand service court, so called because an "ad" score is served there.

All. An even score: 30-all, 3-all, etc.

Alley. The area on either side of the singles court that enlarges the width of the court for doubles. Each alley is $4\frac{1}{2}$ feet wide.

American twist. A spin serve that causes the ball to bounce high and in the opposite direction from which it was originally traveling.

Angle shot. A ball hit to an extreme angle across the court.

Approach. A shot behind which a player comes to the net.

Attack drive. An aggressive approach shot.

Australian doubles. Doubles in which the point begins with the server and server's partner on the same right or left side of the court.

Backcourt. The area between the service line and the baseline.

Backhand. The stroke used to return balls hit to the left of a right-handed player or to the right of a left-handed player.

Backhand court. For a right-handed player, the left-hand side of the court; for a left-handed player, the right-hand side of the court.

Backspin. The ball spins from bottom to top, applied by hitting down and through the ball. Also called "underspin." *See also* Slice, Chop.

Backswing. The initial part of any swing. The act of bringing the racket back to prepare for the forward swing.

Ball person. During competition, a person who retrieves balls for the players.

Baseline. The end boundary line of a tennis court, located 39 feet from the net.

Bevel. The tilt or slant of the racket face.

Boron. The most expensive material used to manufacture racket frames. Extremely durable.

Break service. To win a game in which the opponent serves.

Bye. In competition, the situation in which a player is not required to play in a particular round.

Cannonball. A hard, flat serve.

Center mark. The short line that bisects the center of the baseline.

Center service line. The line that is perpendicular to the net and divides the two service courts.

Center strap. A strap in the center of the net, anchored to the ground to hold the net secure at a height of 3 feet.

Chip. A modified slice, used primarily in doubles to return a serve. A chip requires a short swing, which allows the receiver to move in close to return.

Choke. To grip the racket up higher on the handle.

Chop. A backspin shot in which the racket moves down through the ball at an angle greater than 45 degrees.

Closed face. The angle of the hitting face of the racket when it is turned down toward the court.

Composite. A racket frame reinforced with graphite, fiberglass, or boron.

Consolation. A tournament in which first-round losers continue to play in a losers' tournament.

Cross-court shot. A shot in which the ball travels diagonally across the net, from one corner of the court to the other.

Deep shot. A shot that bounces near the baseline (near the service line on a serve).

Default. Failure to complete a scheduled match in a tournament; a defaulting player forfeits her or his position.

Deuce. A score of 40-40 (the score is tied and each side has at least three points).

Deuce court. Right-hand court, so called because on a deuce score the ball is served there.

Dink. A ball returned so it floats across the net with extreme softness.

Double elimination. A tournament in which a player or team must lose twice before being eliminated.

Double fault. The failure of both service attempts to be good. It costs a point.

Doubles. A game or match with four players, two on each team.

Draw. The means of establishing who plays whom in a tournament.

Drive. An offensive ball hit with force.

Drop shot. A softly hit shot that barely travels over the net.

Drop volley. A drop shot that is volleyed before it bounces.

Earned point. A point won through skillful playing rather than through an opponent's mistake.

Elimination. A tournament in which one is eliminated when defeated.

Error. A point achieved through an obvious mistake rather than through skillful playing.

Face. The hitting surface of the racket.

Fast court. A court with a smooth surface, which allows the ball to bounce quickly and low.

Fault. An improper hit, generally thought of as a service error.

Fifteen. The name of the first point won by a player or team.

Flat shot. A shot that travels in a straight line with little arc and little spin.

Floater. A ball that moves slowly across the net in a high trajectory.

Foot fault. A fault resulting from the server's stepping on or over the baseline before hitting the ball during the serve, or from a player's standing beyond the sideline or touching the wrong side of the center mark before the ball is served.

Forcing shot. A ball hit with exceptional power. A play in which, because of the speed and placement of the shot, the opponent is pulled out of position.

Forecourt. The area between the net and the service line.

Forehand. The stroke used to return balls hit to the right of a right-handed player or to the left of a left-handed player.

Forehand court. For a right-handed player, the right-hand side of the court; for a left-handed player, the left-hand side of the court.

Forty. The score when a player or team has won three points.

Frame. The part of the racket that holds the strings.

Game. That part of a set that is completed when one player or side wins four points, or wins two consecutive points after deuce.

Graphite. Expensive fibers used to produce extra-strength racket frames.

Grip. The method of holding the racket handle. The term given the leather covering on the handle.

Groundstroke. Forehand or backhand stroke made after the ball has bounced.

Gut. Racket strings made from animal intestines.

Half volley. Hitting the ball immediately after it bounces off the court.

Handle. The part of the racket that is gripped in the hand.

Head. The part of the racket used to hit the ball; includes the frame and the strings.

Hold serve. To win a game in which one was server.

Kill. To smash the ball down hard.

Large head. The largest available racket frame size.

Let. A point replayed because of interference. A serve that hits the top of the net but is otherwise good.

Linesperson. In competition, a person responsible for calling balls that land outside the court.

Lob. A ball hit high enough in the air to clear the net, usually by at least 10 feet, and to pass over the head of the net player.

Love. Zero; no score.

Love game. A game won without the winner's losing a point.

Love set. A set won without the winner's losing a game.

Match. Singles or doubles play consisting of two out of three sets for all women's and most men's matches, or three out of five sets for many men's championship matches.

Match point. The game point that, if won, also will win the match for a player or team.

Midcourt. The general area in the center of the playing court, midway between the net and baseline.

Mid-size. A medium-size racket head; larger than a conventional head, but smaller than a large head.

Mix up. To vary the types of shots attempted.

Net game. The play at net. Also called "net play."

Net person. A player positioned at the net.

No ad. Scoring system in which the first player or team to score four points wins the game.

No-man's-land. Midcourt, where many balls bounce at the player's feet and the player is unusually vulnerable.

Nylon. A type of synthetic racket string.

Open face. The angle of the hitting face of the racket when it is turned up, away from the court surface.

Opening. A defensive mistake that allows an opponent a good chance to score a point.

Out. A ball landing outside the playing court.

Overhead smash. See Smash.

Oversized. Refers to mid-size or large racket heads. Larger than the conventional racket head.

Overspin. See Topspin.

Pace. The speed or spin of a ball, which makes it bounce quickly.

Passing shot. A ball hit out of reach of a net player.

Percentage tennis. "Conservative" tennis that emphasizes cutting down on unnecessary errors and on errors at critical points.

Place. To hit the ball to a desired area.

Placement. A shot placed so accurately that an opponent cannot be expected to return it.

Poach. A doubles strategy in which the net player moves over to the partner's side of the court to make a volley.

Press. A wooden frame that holds a wood tennis racket firmly so as to prevent it from warping when not in use.

Rally. Play in exclusion of the serve.

Retrieve. A good return of a difficult shot.

Round-robin. A tournament in which every player plays every other player.

Rush. To advance to the net after hitting an approach shot.

Seed. To arrange tournament matches so that top players don't play each other until the final rounds.

Serve (Service). Method of starting a point.

Service line. The line that marks the base of the service court; parallel to the baseline and 21 feet from the net.

Set. That part of a match that is completed when one player or side wins at least six games and is ahead by at least two games, or has won the tie break.

Set point. The game point that, if won, also will win the set for a player or team.

Sidespin. A shot in which the ball spins to the side and bounces to the side. The sidespin slice is one of the most common types of serve.

Singles. A match between two players.

Slice. A backspin shot hit with the racket traveling down through the ball at less than a 45-degree angle with the ground. *See also* Chip.

Slow court. A court with a rough surface, which tends to make the ball bounce rather high and slow.

Smash. A hard-hit overhead shot.

Spin. Rotation of the ball caused by hitting it at an angle. See Topspin, Sidespin, Backspin.

Straight sets. To win a match without the winner's losing a set.

Sudden death. In no-ad scoring, when the score reaches 3-all.

Synthetic gut. A racket "string" composed of several fibers of a synthetic material (not actually gut) twisted together.

Tape. The fabric band that stretches across the top of the net. The lines of a clay court.

Tennis elbow. A painful condition of the elbow joint commonly caused by hyperextension of the elbow or by excessive wrist action in tennis play.

Thirty. The score when a player or team has won two points.

Throat. The part of the racket between the handle and the head.

Tie breaker. When the score in any set reaches 6 games all, a 12-point scoring system is used to determine the winner of the set.

Topspin. Spin of the ball from top to bottom, caused by hitting up and through the ball. It makes the ball bounce fast and long and is used on most groundstrokes.

Trajectory. The flight of the ball in relation to the top of the net.

Umpire. The person who officiates at major matches.

Undercut. A backspin caused by hitting down through the ball.

Underspin. See Backspin, Slice, Chop.

Unseeded. The players not favored to win nor given any special place on draw in a tournament.

VASSS. A no-ad, sudden-death game scoring system.

Volley. To hit the ball before it bounces.

Wood shot. A ball hit on the edge—rather than the face—of a wood racket.